THE LANDSCAPE OF
LONDON

SAMPSON LLOYD
CAMERON BROWN

THE LANDSCAPE OF LONDON

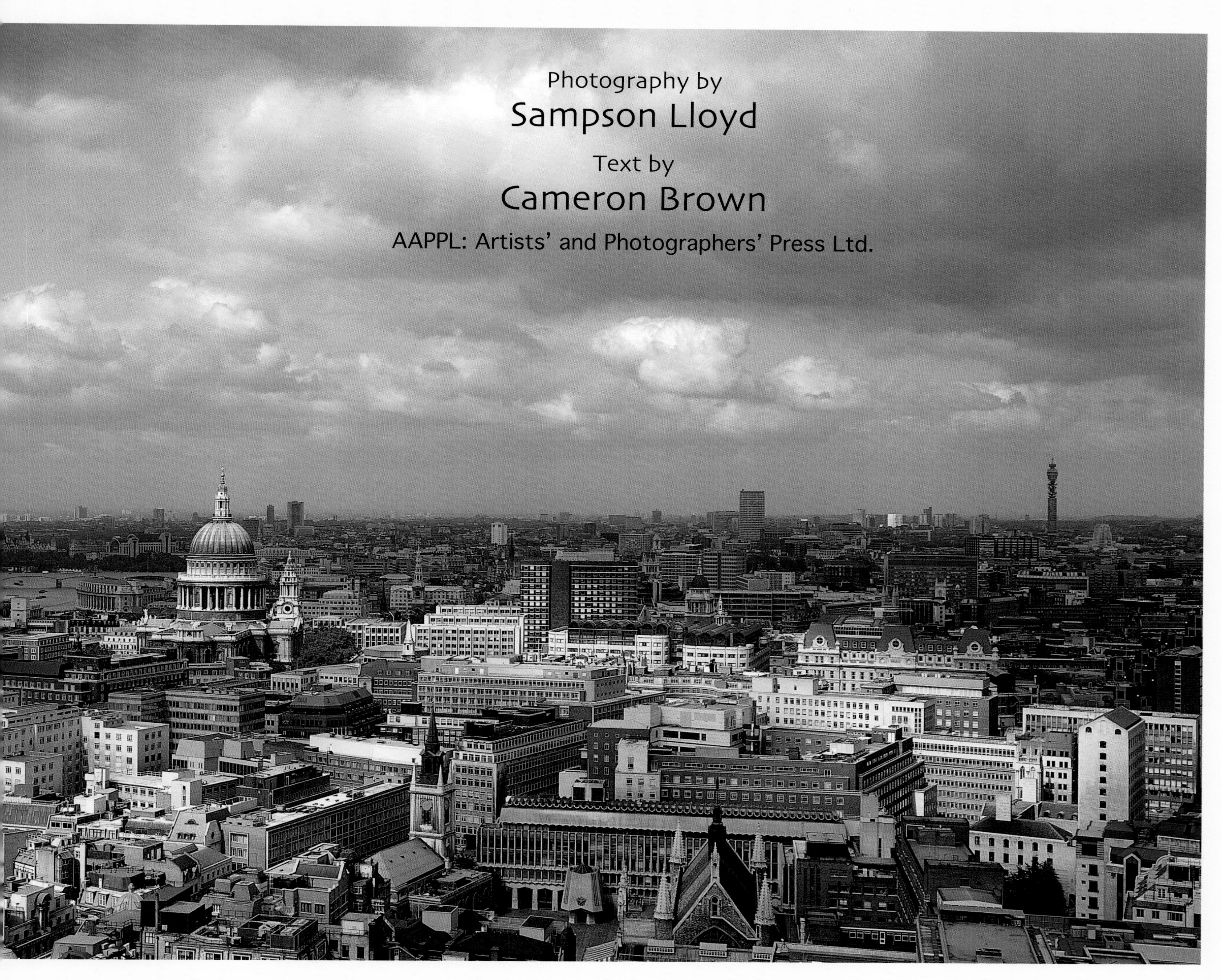

Photography by
Sampson Lloyd

Text by
Cameron Brown

AAPPL: Artists' and Photographers' Press Ltd.

THE LANDSCAPE OF LONDON

Published by
AAPPL Artists' and Photographers' Press Ltd.
10 Hillside London SW19 4NH
info@aappl.com
www.aappl.com

Sales and Distribution
UK and export: Turnaround Publisher Services Ltd.
Unit 3 Olympia Business Park, Coburg Rd., London N22 6TZ
orders@turnaround-uk.com

A catalogue record for this book is available from the British Library.

ISBN 1-904332-43-9 EAN 9781904332435

Art Director and Designer: Stefan Nekuda
s.nekuda@chello.at

Reproduction and printing by: Imago Publishing
info@imago.co.uk

Half title page: No 1 London Bridge
Title page: View from Drapers Gardens

Contents

London, an Introduction

The great sprawl of modern London seen from the window of a plane passing over on its way to Heathrow offers a swathe of red and grey roofs, patches of green and a meandering river. There is quantity in evidence but little hint of quality. The visitor may get a glimpse of the Palace of Westminster, with St. James's Park behind and the elegant London Eye before; he may see the squat features of the Millennium Dome and the elegance of Greenwich just across the muddy Thames. Even when he has landed and reaches the city itself, unless he knows where to look and how to look he will see only fragments of London's turbulent history, of its vibrant commercial life, its proud traditions and the architectural splendours, sacred and secular, tucked away in its unassuming streets and its historic "villages". In its layout London is one of the world's more chaotic cities, one which has evolved rather than been designed, its constituent parts self-contained, each proud in some way of its own character; the institutions – monarchy, government, church, the law, commerce – evolving at different paces and in different places. London boasts few grand and opulent buildings but has hundreds which, on a more modest scale, tell us of its history. Westminster Abbey, one of the grand few and built over a 500 year period, is a history lesson in itself, and one which is seen by most visitors (and probably quite a few Londoners); but how many stray into the peaceful medieval squares of the Inner Temple, or look behind the doors of the City's 50-odd churches nestling with dignity amongst the finest and most confident examples of modern secular architecture? Which of them think about the stories behind the names of streets such as Cheapside, Houndsditch or Pall Mall? How many know that there is a Victorian pedestrian tunnel running under the river from the Isle of Dogs to Greenwich?

Sampson Lloyd's photography takes us on a journey through our capital: a journey in time as well as space. He has an eye for the detail as much as for the big picture. This is a photography book whose images will add something to the reader's understanding and enjoyment of London but it cannot pretend to be a comprehensive guide; the subject is far too big for a single book. The text is here simply to help the fan of Sampson Lloyd's photography place the images in some sort of historical context.

The Romans could be said to have founded London although there is evidence that people lived in the area long before 43AD when Aulus Plautius led his invasion. Julius Caesar had been in England already, leaving some 90 years earlier, but he did not seem to have built at London. When this next wave of Roman invaders arrived they will have marched through Kent towards Colchester, the most important city of the era. The Thames was wide and wooded and the soldiers, rather than searching for a ford, will have had recourse to the surrounding forests for the material to build a bridge. Recent excavations by the Thames show that a wooden bridge was built around 2,000 years ago, close to where London Bridge stands today.

The first Palace of Westminster was built on the north bank of the Thames by Edward the Confessor in the 11th century. Today's parliament buildings were opened almost exactly 800 years later and are home to the House of Commons and The House of Lords.

The Romans settled on the north bank and called the new town Londinium. Despite the efforts of the warrior-queen Boudicca, who, within 20 years of their arrival had burned their new settlement to the ground and killed or evicted large numbers of inhabitants, the Romans stayed and rebuilt and the city prospered under their rule for the best part of 400 years.

The Romans were soldiers and traders and London proved an ideal focal point for defence and, because of its river and relative closeness to the sea, for transportation. As the invaders became more settled their trading patterns evolved; becoming more self-sufficient and less reliant upon imports of basic goods – foodstuffs, clothing, tools – they expanded their trade with the local tribes and established Londinium as a commercial centre too. The history of the Roman era is well-documented. As their empire flourished so too did London, its population rising to perhaps 40-45,000 at its peak, but as the Empire began to have its troubles troops

(right) Archeological evidence proves that there has been human settlement in and around the London area for thousands of years. The earliest remaining evidence of permanent settlement in what now comprises the city dates from the Roman era and fragments of the city wall can still be seen, here close to the Tower of London.

and administrators were called away and London's importance to the Romans began to wane. By early in the 5th century they had gone and London went into the least documented period of its history.

The next few centuries saw attacks and invasions from Saxons, Danes and Norwegians. From place names alone it is clear that the Saxons moved their settlement west of the Roman city to the area around The Strand and Aldwych: *aeld wyc* is Saxon for "old town" and the suffix lives on in many other northern and eastern towns – Ipswich, Norwich, Nantwich and so on. Christianity had been introduced during the Roman period and around 604AD the first St. Paul's Cathedral was built, on the site occupied by the present St. Paul's. By the 9th century London had regained its position as a prosperous trading centre and much of the populace had moved back into the walled area of Londinium or, as the Saxons named it, Ludenwic. As was ever the story, wealth attracted attention, and in 851 a raiding party of Danish Vikings sailed up the Thames and plundered and burned the city. By the late years of the 9th century Alfred the Great had ousted the Danes but within a few years of his death they were back.

One hundred years later it was the Anglo-Saxons and Norwegian Vikings raiding London and destroying London Bridge in a series of attacks which were only halted when the Danish King Cnut (usually known here as Canute) came to power in 1017. He managed to unite the Danes with the Anglo-Saxons, as much through the mutual benefits of commerce as through force, but after his death control reverted to the Anglo-Saxon King Edward ("The Confessor"). At his death in 1065 King Harold came to the throne and was famously killed at the Battle of Hastings just one year later and so London entered its next period of relative stability under the Normans.

When William the Conqueror invaded, London was the most prosperous and the largest city - but it was not the capital of the realm. The official seat of government was at Winchester, although the royal residence was generally at London. St. Paul's had been rebuilt again after its destruction by the Vikings and Edward the Confessor had built a substantial monastery and church upriver from the Roman and Saxon settlements, at Westminster. King Harold had broken with tradition by having himself crowned at the new Westminster Abbey, and on Christmas Day 1066 William the Conqueror celebrated his own coronation there and so cemented the shift of temporal as well as ecclesiastical power to London.

Within one generation the Normans instigated fundamental changes, the legacy of which is with us today. William I started building the Tower of London, a

In common with the docks and warehouses, the power stations along the Thames have one by one been converted to new use. Bankside power station became Tate Modern but the iconic Battersea power station has yet to find a new use.

massive fortress at the south-east corner of the old city, and just beyond the boundary marked by the Roman wall; the merchants and citizens of London were being shown in no uncertain terms who was in charge. Initially The Tower was also the royal residence but by the end of the century William II had started building Westminster Hall, next to the Abbey, to provide the new seat of government. Thus began a period of tension and sometimes hostility between the monarchy and the commercial interests of the city and when William's brother Henry succeeded him he was forced to buy support from the city by granting the locals the right to raise direct taxes. The king was recognising that power lay not only with the monarch and his army but with the financial power-brokers of the day. In 1192 the first Mayor of London was elected, a position which lives on today as The Lord Mayor of London.

So began the inexorable rise of the City of London, the financial district, the "square mile", which still occupies the 600-odd acres of the Roman City but which through its broad range of financial services is the single largest contributor to the modern British economy.

By 1176 the population of London was not yet back to the level it had reached under the Romans, and the first stone bridge was built over the Thames. Because of the importance of this bridge to the city authorities as a tax-generator it remained the only permanent crossing downriver of Kingston until the 18th century. The tax on shipments of coal through London Bridge financed much of the rebuilding of the city after the Great Fire of London in 1666.

The river was the site of great buildings: the Palace of Westminster, the Tower, Greenwich Palace and Hampton Court. In those days of unmetalled roads and poor street lighting the river was often the only safe way to travel and ferrymen provided one of the few means of public transport. The Thames was the oil in the machinery of trade and by the mid-nineteenth century 25% of all Londoners were employed in shipping, in the docks or in other, related industries.

Medieval London was still substantially bounded by the borders of the Roman city, with important developments at Westminster a few miles upriver and the beginnings of the movement of population to the "old town" along the Strand and to the fields east and north of the city wall. London at the time was a maze of twisting streets and lanes with wooden, limewashed houses constantly threatened by fire. As early as the 13th century a law was passed requiring new houses to use slate rather than thatched roofs, but it seems this may have been ignored and in consequence most of the city was burned down in 1666. What lends the City (the financial district) much of its character today is that it was rebuilt on the old street plan. Christopher Wren would gladly have started again and had planned a

The absolute rule of kings and queens of England has been tested and gradually reduced ever since the introduction of the concept of *aldermen* in the ninth century. But even today reminders of the wealth and privelege surrounding the royal family abound.

Traditional ceremony continues to play a part in London's daily life. Here the Royal Horse Artillery, in dress uniform, put on a display in Hyde Park.

much more formal city along classical lines, with vistas and avenues, but no-one then had the power to simply overrule the interests of the landowners in the area who would have been deeply affected by such a scheme. Thus today's visitor can still wander the medieval streets and imagine the old bakeries of Pudding Lane and Bread Street, the markets in Poultry and Milk Street or the tailors of Threadneedle Street. Wealthy landowners built near The Strand and lawyers congregated around the Inns of Court off Fleet Street and Grays Inn, and so began the tendency to keep moving outwards which eventually led to the urban and suburban sprawl of London's 32 boroughs and 8 million residents at the beginning of the 21st century.

The earliest surviving map of London, by the engraver Frans Honenberg, shows the town of around 1550. The population at the time was about 90,000 and most of the buildings are still firmly within the square mile, bounded to the north and east by a city wall with an outer ditch running right up to the moated Tower at the south-east corner. There are small settlements at "Spital Field" and "Smyth Field" to the north of the wall, and again just to the east of The Tower. The Strand, the highway linking the city to Westminster, has housing on both sides, but everything further north and beyond Charing Cross (today's Trafalgar Square) is fields. Across London Bridge Southwark is populated but barely a few streets from the river the fields begin again. There is only one bridge and the river is shown teeming with boats and ferries of all sizes.

The great periods of speculative building were in the 18th and early 19th centuries, on estates owned by wealthy families such as the Grosvenors and Cadogans, whose names live on today in the streets of Mayfair and Chelsea. John Nash was another of the great builders who transformed Regent's Park from derelict scrubland into one of London's most sought-after residential areas and created Regent Street, separating Covent Garden from Soho. The coming of the railway age in the 1830s drew into the city those villages which had seemed far removed from town

Cesar Ritz worked at the Savoy (above right) to earn the money to open his eponymous Hotel. In Savoy Street traffic must drive on the right, a legacy of the time when horse-drawn carriages found it easier to make an anti-clockwise turn at the hotel entrance.

With over 7.5 million inhabitants London faces transport challenges. The city was not designed for vehicular traffic and today's commuter is increasingly encouraged to walk or cycle or to travel by train, tube or the familiar red bus.

to create rapidly-growing sources of modestly-priced suburban housing for commuters. London has spread without smothering and the individual character of many of its constituent parts remains to this day. Hoxton is not like Hampstead, nor Chelsea like Clerkenwell. Despite the relative ease of travel today, north of the river and south of the river remain two distinct worlds, at least to those who live there ...

The 20th century brought the ravages of war and the almost comparable destruction wrought by the planners and developers of the 1960s. The docks died, Docklands was born and Londoners rediscovered the delights of their river, as docks, warehouses and wharves were redeveloped or cleared to make way for new flats, shops and offices with a view of the water.

Today's town-dweller entertains himself in much the same way as his relatives did one, two or three centuries before. The rowdy gardens and bear-baiting pits of Vauxhall may have yielded to the clubs and cinemas of Soho and the West End but there are still the theatres, the markets, the pubs and the parks. For a city of its size and population density London has an astonishing number of public green spaces, ranging from lowly Victorian municipal gardens to the Royal Parks and the commons dotted around the suburbs. London breathes: it has parks everywhere, eight of them created half a millennium ago by the Kings of England keen to hunt deer on their

doorstep. But away from these grand open spaces Londoners have preserved smaller oases in churchyards and local parks, squares and gardens. Londoners love to work in their own gardens or just relax in the park and can enjoy the outdoors much more since the clean air act of the 1950s spelled the end of the deadly London smog. It had taken the "Great Stink" of 1858, when even Parliament had to suspend sittings because the stench from the Thames was so foul, to inconvenience enough important people that something was finally done about the sewage problem. In the same way it took 2000 deaths in one bout of smog in 1953 to spell the end of that atmosphere so beloved of old films and still imagined by some visitors to be typical of London today.

The face of London is always changing. Immigration of the unfriendly kind created a population melded from Norsemen and Celts, Vikings, Romans and Normans. As political and religious persecution took place all around Europe in the middle ages and later, and conflict and famine drove people from their homes, London saw the arrival of Jews and Huguenots, Irish and Scots, Russians and Cypriots and, in the second half of the 20th century economic immigrants from the old Commonwealth countries and refugees from wars and civil disturbance throughout the world. London is truly a multi-cultured multi-ethnic city today and the influence of immigration is there in our townscape, our cuisine and our language. London would be inconceivable without its Ugandan-Asian corner-shops, Caribbean bus-drivers or Australian barmen, to say nothing of its Chinese and Indian (or, more often, Bengali) restaurants, its Turkish doner-kebabs and Greek-Cypriot fish and chip shops. Sampson Lloyd has captured the essence of the city in this fine collection of photographs.

The parents of many of today's Londoners came from the former British Commonwealth. London was always *the* destination for refugees and for what we now call economic migrants. Each wave of immigrants leaves its permanent mark on the culture of the capital.

The River

Tower Bridge is the last example of the wave of Victorian bridge-building. Opened in 1894, it was the first bridge ever built down-river from London Bridge.

From its source at Thames Head off the Fosse Way, the Roman Road from Bath to Cirencester, to the estuary and the North Sea, the Thames winds its way for some 215 miles. The upper part of the river was known to the Romans as Isis; the lower part as Tamesis. In Celtic the two were called *Taom* and *Uis* and the modern name Thames clearly has its roots somewhere in this Romano-Celtic past.

The city of London was probably founded by the Romans some time between 54BC, when Caesar departed for the second time, and the next Roman invasion some 90 years later. It was not the Roman's principle settlement and it is possible that it was simply a convenient place at which to ford the river on the journey north from Kent to Colchester. The river then would be unrecognizable today; much wider – perhaps as much as a mile at Westminster - shallower and slower-flowing, and bordered by marsh and woodland. Unattractive as this sounds it was clearly recognisable as a key point of access to central and southern England for both military and trading purposes, as well as a constant source of food. The Thames of 2000 years ago teemed with fish – salmon, trout, eels – all of which provided staples in the diet of the locals until well into the 19th century.

Little is known of life in London between the departure of the Romans in 410 AD and the arrival of the Norman conquerors 656 years later. The Vikings and Saxons, invading during this period, used the Thames as a means of access and built on both north and south banks of the estuary, though the Saxons seem to have settled and built their town in the area west of the Roman city, closer to today's Strand. It seems that the Roman bridge had been lost or destroyed and without a bridge across the Thames the river will have reverted to being as much a barrier as a trade route.

William of Normandy did not invade via the Thames but, like the invaders before him, recognized the strategic importance of London. The Romans had built defensive fortifications near the site of The Tower of London and the Normans extended the network of castles all over their new kingdom, including Windsor on the Thames. Later on the Tudors, living in constant fear of invasions from France or Spain added defences East of London at Tilbury, Woolwich and Sheerness.

Not surprisingly many of the great royal palaces – Windsor Castle, Hampton Court, Whitehall and Greenwich – as well as major Church and State buildings – Westminster Abbey, The House of Lords, St. Paul's – were all built along the river. Stone and timber could be brought in, in the case of The Tower and Westminster Abbey from the Normans' own homeland and the "important people" could travel safely and comfortably on the river in an era when roads were dangerous, uncomfortable and in winter sometimes impassable. This coming together of royalty and government, church and commerce along a relatively short stretch of the river provides much of the reason for London's dominance in what now comprises the United Kingdom.

For many people over the ages the river has been their livelihood, whether as fishermen or laudrywomen, millers or bargees, lockkeepers or smugglers. The river is tidal up to Teddington and before the construction of the locks, beginning in the 17th century, navigation was sometimes unpredictable. The first lock was built in 1630 at Abingdon and by the end of the 18th century there was easy travel up and down much of the length of the river. The most impressive of these man-made devices to control the river's flow is surely the Thames barrier below Greenwich, built to prevent the serious flooding which could occur in central London following particularly high tides in the North Sea.

The advent of the railways in the 1830s spelled the beginning of the end for the Thames' upriver commercial use; the railways were simply more efficient than horse-drawn barges. The river above Teddington changed in character, becoming a recreational waterway for the middle and upper classes, and at the same time the character of the rest of the river was changing equally dramatically. In the east the docks were growing apace whilst in central London the Victorians were indulging in a frenzy of bridge-building.

The first stone bridge over the Thames, Old London Bridge, was started in 1176 and took over 30 years to complete. It had 19 arches built so close together that it caused serious turbulence and prevented larger ships from passing upriver. Just as with today's Tower Bridge, a drawbridge was built into the middle and a toll charged to any ship needing to have the bridge opened. The tax on wool being exported via this bridge became a huge source of revenue for the City of London. Even by the early 18th century this overcrowded structure, covered in shops and houses and crammed with traffic was the only Thames crossing below Kingston, several miles upriver. The most convenient way for most people to cross the river was by boat and the watermen and ferries provided the capital's chief form of public transport. A bridge at Westminster to replace the horse-ferry was proposed as early as 1664 but the vested interests in the City, deriving vast revenues from London Bridge, effectively bribed the king with a £100,000 "loan" to reject the proposal and it was not until 1729 that London's second bridge was built at Fulham. Westminster Bridge was finally opened in 1750, the monopoly of the watermen and ferrymen was broken and the door was opened for the construction of further bridges.

London was growing rapidly and traffic congestion was as severe as today so further bridges were needed to keep trade and workers moving across the capital. The houses on Old London Bridge were finally demolished in 1762 and the roadway widened. The neighbouring Blackfriars Bridge opened in 1768 and Battersea Bridge followed in 1776. Vauxhall Bridge, the first cast-iron bridge across the Thames was built in 1816, Waterloo Bridge in 1817 and Southwark Bridge in 1819. In 1827 London's first suspension bridge was built at Hammersmith and plans were under way to demolish Old London Bridge. It finally came down in 1831 when a new London Bridge was opened. Old London Bridge managed to stand for around 700 years but not one of the bridges built between the mid 18th and mid 19th centuries has survived without rebuilding at least once. The Victorians added Albert Bridge, Chelsea Bridge, Wandsworth Bridge and, most famously, the last of the Victorian bridges, Tower Bridge, opened in 1894, and now one of the most well-known icons of London. In its early years its steam-driven drawbridge would open up to 50 times a day to let ships pass through.

Old paintings often depict grand fairs and other entertainments on the banks of the river and even on the river itself; when the Thames froze sufficiently hard the famous Frost Fairs were held. Stalls were erected on the frozen river, fires lit and oxen roasted. There were fairgrounds, dancing bears, and all the hustle and bustle of the fairground and all upon the ice. The last one took place in 1814 but the fact that the river never seems to freeze over today (the last time was in 1963, and then not nearly severely enough for a Frost Fair) is not just because of global warming. In 1858 the effects of pollution, caused mainly by untreated sewage and industrial effluent discharged into the river, were so awful that a sitting of Parliament had to be suspended. This became known as The Great Stink and led to the government

Blackfriars was the third Thames bridge and was started in 1760. The present bridge opened in 1869.

Looking northwest from Tower Bridge, the girders frame one of the City's newest buildings, "The Gherkin"

The first Lambeth Bridge was opened in 1862 at a river-crossing which had been used by ferryman since the early 1500s. The present steel bridge replaced the Victorian structure in 1932.

The footbridge at Waterloo provides some of the finest views up and down river. The nearby road bridge was opened in 1817 and given its name to commemorate Wellington's victory at Waterloo in 1815. It has subsequently given its name to the whole area.

of the day deciding to invest in a new underground sewage system for London. As part of this process embankments were built which narrowed the river considerably, thus increasing the speed of its flow and making freezing less likely. A further consequence of the construction of the new embankments was the loss of many of the tributaries which had fed the metropolitan Thames for centuries. It is not easy to "lose" a river and, in fact, many were redirected into the new sewage system or into conduits, flowing eventually back into the Thames, but they were lost to sight. The old Westbourne, for instance, now flows underground, passing at one stage through an iron conduit which can be seen under the roof of Chelsea's Sloane Square tube station.

The docks retained their commercial importance until well into the 1960s when a combination of the growth of container shipping, the sheer size of modern tankers and liners and the debilitating effects of the restrictive trade practices of the dockers led to a swift and inevitable decline in the activities of the Port of London. Where cranes once filled the skyline of the Isle of Dogs there are now the dominating towers of Canary Wharf, the new home of London's international trade, now in financial services rather than tea, spices or coal.

The Romans, inevitably, created the first real port here, on the north bank of the river and traded actively with their far-flung colonies, bringing into London wine, oils, fruit, salt, spices and luxury goods, and exporting slaves, animal-skins and other "basic" goods. As they became more established here they imported less from abroad and expanded domestic trade, shipping goods around the British coasts and up the river. In the Middle Ages the most important export was wool. Dick Whittington, famous Lord Mayor of London, was a mercer and exporter of woollen cloth. Coal was the next dominant commodity and taxes on coal shipped through London Bridge paid for the rebuilding of the city after the Great Fire of 1666. Even at this time it is estimated that a quarter of the population of London were employed in shipping. What seagoing trade remains today - and there is still a good deal that cannot be moved economically by air or by truck - has been pushed east to Tilbury and Sheerness or even out to Rotterdam. The boats to be seen passing Tower Bridge in the early 21st century will be carrying tourists, not coal.

In the dramatic light of the evening sun and with the backdrop of a stormy sky, the Albert Bridge retains its almost frivolous attractiveness. Opened in 1873 it is one of several London landmarks named in honour of Queen Victoria's late consort.

The Millennium Dome at Greenwich cost £750 million to complete and remained open for just one year.

Albert Bridge, a highly ornamented cantilevered suspension bridge was strength[illegible] in 1973 to cope with [illegible] traffic.

The phone box and the Battersea power station, seen here from Albert Bridge, are both designs of Giles Gilbert Scott.

The Millennium Bridge from Tate Modern to St. Paul's was closed for 18 months when first opened in 2000, because it wobbled

(next page) Battersea power station opened in 1933 and closed exactly 50 years later. It is destined to become a leisure complex

All along the metropolitan Thames are moorings
for retired scientific, naval and pleasure boats.

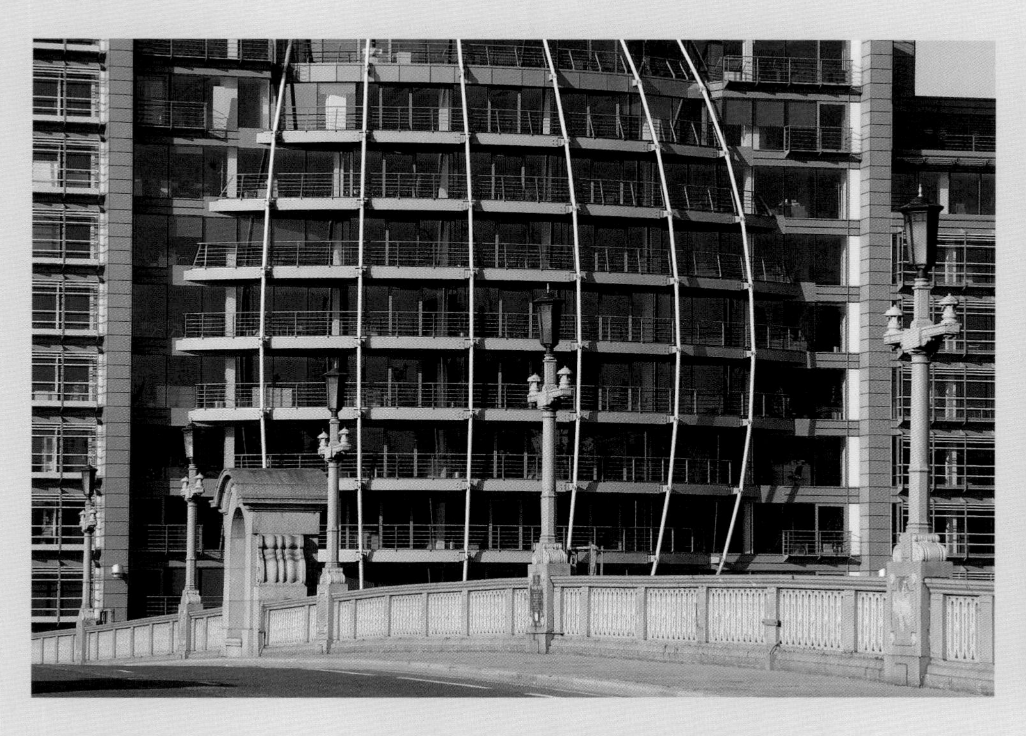

Glass, steel and concrete homes for the 21st Century at the southern end of Southwark Bridge.

The MI6 building on the south bank at Vauxhall Bridge was designed by Terry Farrell and Associates and opened in 1993.

St. Katharine's Dock next to the Tower of London was one of the first examples of how derelict warehouses could be redeveloped.

Looking south east from Tower Bridge, former warehouses and factories have been converted into flats and offices.

This statue of Queen Victoria seems to be taking a stroll across Blackfriars Bridge ...

Chelsea Harbour, seen here from Battersea, is one of London's few successful high-rise residential developments.

Getting to your houseboat can be a complicated process and can mean disturbing the neighbours.

Only 50 years ago the river supported tens of thousands of jobs. With the demise of the docks few working boats remain.

Greenwich Palace, favourite home of three generations of monarchs, was demolished in 1694 to make way for Wren's Royal Naval College.

If sea levels continue to rise at the present rate the Thames Barrier, completed in 1982, will only protect London from flooding until around 2030.

Downriver from Tower Bridge a jumble of old warehouse buildings has found new life as flats for City workers, with converted barges in the foreground.

Battersea Bridge first opened in 1772. Here the 1890 replacement is seen with Chelsea Harbour in the background.

(next page) The trees of Cheyne Walk, Chelsea, frame a peaceful river scene, looking across to Battersea Park.

HMS Belfast, launched in 1938, saw service in World War II and the Korean War. She has been open to the public since 1971.

(next page) Upriver at Richmond, Surrey, the Thames takes on a distinctly pastoral character.

History and Tradition

Echoes of London's past are to be found throughout the capital, from the fragments of the old Roman wall and remnants of Saxon church buildings, to the very street-names of much of the city. Statues throughout London keep us in mind of past military conquests and scientific and humanitarian achievement. The quirky customs and practices maintained in London's institutions, schools, clubs and professions remind Londoners that they are part of a unique society. But London does not always wear its history on its sleeve. Few of its great buildings look as they did when first built and many of them take a little finding. The history and even the grandeur is there, however, and London is the equal of any city in the preservation and enjoyment of traditions at all levels and in all parts of society. At one end of the social scale is all that which is associated with the monarchy: the changing of the guard, trooping the colour, Beefeaters at The Tower; there is a parliament whose members are not allowed to address each other by name, judges and lawyers in powdered wigs, and unarmed policemen. There are the Summer Exhibition, the Chelsea Flower Show, Wimbledon, Henley and Ascot. At a more down-to-earth level are school uniforms, milkmen delivering to the front door and black cabs.

Grand buildings are not found in one area alone though there are inevitable concentrations; for instance, most of the finest and oldest ecclesiastical architecture is within the square mile of the City of London. For visual pomp, however, there is nothing to match the Palace of Westminster (Houses of Parliament) together with its neighbour, Westminster Abbey. Though parts of both of these buildings are of considerable age – the Great Hall of the Palace of Westminster dating back to the 12th century and the Abbey to the 13th - what catches the eye today is rather more recent. The twin towers of the Abbey are an 18th century addition and the pinnacles are Victorian. The Houses of Parliament are now almost wholly Victorian, a fire having destroyed all but the Great Hall on October 16th 1834. Big Ben itself was finished as recently as 1860.

Another iconic edifice, The Tower of London, has, by contrast, stood sentinel at the eastern end of the City for almost 1,000 years. Started by William I in 1078 and finished 200 years later by Edward I this 18 acre complex has served variously as fortress, palace, prison, place of execution, mint, observatory, record office and home to the Crown Jewels. The Beefeaters, more correctly known as Yeoman Warders of The Tower, still wear the red uniforms from the time of their formation by Edward VI in the mid 16th century. Today's Beefeaters are all former members of the army or airforce.

Queen Victoria moved into the newly-rebuilt Buckingham Palace in 1837. The building has 600 rooms, of which only a dozen or so are for the private use of the Queen and the Duke of Edinburgh.

Henry VIII broke with tradition by moving his court downriver to Greenwich. The present symmetrical Italianate structure is of later date and is the work of a number of fine architects: Inigo Jones, Wren, Hawksmoor and Vanbrugh. What a striking contrast this must have made when it was first built, to the red-brick, turreted style of the palaces of Hampton Court or St James's and how different to have a London building of this scale planned and built with such symmetry and homogeneity of style. It is on the site of the Queen's House at Greenwich that Sir Walter Raleigh is said to have laid his cloak across a puddle so that Queen Elizabeth would not get mud on the royal feet.

St. Paul's is the only major London church building to have been designed and built in a uniform style. In 1663 Wren had started work on the redesign of the old cathedral which then fell victim to the ravages of the Great Fire of London only 3 years later. Not unusually for London the present magnificent building sits on the site of its medieval forerunners, hemmed in by buildings, rather than being surrounded and shown off by its own piazza. It does however form an integral part of the London skyline when seen from the Thames and readily justifies the words on Wren's tomb in the crypt of St. Paul's: *Lector, si monumentum requires, circumspice (reader, if you seek my monument, look around you).*

Buckingham Palace certainly is splendidly located. Its "driveway", The Mall, broad and tree-lined, creates a vista of the royal residence from Trafalgar Square, three quarters of a mile away. Its "front gardens" are St. James' Park and Green

Looking across from Greenwich to the towers of Canary Wharf on the Isle of Dogs. The Queen's House in the foreground was completed in the 1630s to a design of Inigo Jones.

Park and it has its own walled "back yard" of over 40 acres. John Sheffield, Duke of Buckingham, was the first to build a house here, in 1702-5. It was bought by George III in 1762 but his son, George IV, who came to the throne in 1820, felt it was not an appropriate palace for a monarch and persuaded parliament to put up £200,000 for a new one. By the time Queen Victoria was finally able to move in 1837 the bill had risen to three times the original estimate, and still the plumbing was not working, bells for the servants were not connected and many of the windows could not be opened. *Plus ca change ...*

The Mall itself is home to a series of fine buildings. St.James's Palace is on the site of a medieval leper hospital, which was bought and demolished by Henry VIII in 1531. It remained the principal royal palace until Queen Victoria moved around the corner to Buckingham Palace. Clarence House, designed by John Nash, whose Regent's Park terraces are amongst London's grandest private homes, is actually connected by a passage to St. James's Palace. Completed in 1828, Princess Anne was born here and in later years it was the home of Queen Elizabeth, the Queen Mother. Parallel to The Mall is the older street of Pall Mall, supposedly named after a French or Italian game *pallo a maglio*, introduced to smart London society by James I in 1603. The street, built in 1662 and originally called Catharine Street, became one of the most sought-after addresses for the rich and fashionable. Most of the great houses, built mainly in the 18th and 19th centuries are home now to gentlemen's clubs such as The Travellers', The Athanaeum and The Carlton.

Just around the corner on Piccadilly is Burlington House. With an unassuming entrance and modest courtyard it is home to the Royal Academy of Arts, founded in 1768. Now the last remaining nobleman's mansion on Piccadilly, Burlington House was completed by the first Earl of Burlington in the 1660s but redesigned in the 18th and 19th centuries. At the western end of Piccadilly, at the entrance to Hyde Park, stands Aspley House, its postal address: No 1, London. Designed by Robert Adam for Lord Bathurst in 1771-8, it became the home of the Duke of Wellington from 1817 until his death in 1852. It now houses the Wellington Museum. Opposite Aspley House, in the middle of London's busiest traffic island, stands Wellington Arch (also called Constitution Arch). The bronze statue on top, *Quadrigia*, the angel of peace, was added as late as 1912 and the foot of the arch used to house a tiny police station.

At the western end of Hyde Park are the Albert Hall and Albert Memorial, Kensington Gardens and Palace, and the mansions of Kensington and Holland Park. The sites for the Albert Hall and the South Kensington museums were acquired at Prince Albert's suggestion in 1852 using profits from the Great Exhibition held in Hyde Park in 1851. The Albert Hall was finally built between 1867 and 1871 and financed from the selling of 999-year leases on 1,300 seats, at a cost of £100 each. This magnificent concert hall can seat 8,000 people and is home to the Promenade season with its world-famous Last Night of the Proms. The Albert Memorial with its exuberant multi-coloured stonework, gilded mosaics and statuary - the pedestal alone is decorated with a frieze of 169 prominent scientists and artists, all life-size - was completed in 1876 and renovated in the late 1990s, at a cost of around £15 million.

The first building on the site of Kensington Palace in the south-west corner of Kensington Gardens was erected early in the 17th century, getting its first royal owner when acquired by William III in 1689. Substantially rebuilt and improved over the years it was the birthplace of Queen Victoria and home to Prince Charles and Diana, Princess of Wales, Princess Margaret, Princess Alice and various other senior members of the Royal Family.

Buckingham Palace is famously protected by the guards and the changing of the guard has become a major tourist attraction. There are seven guards' regiments, the Life Guards, Blues & Royals (these two with plumed metal helmets), the Grenadiers, Coldstream, Scots, Irish and Welsh Guards, all with the equally familiar bearskins. These regiments together are known as the Household Division and all their members are serving soldiers performing normal military roles around the world in addition to their traditional and ceremonial activities. The Sovereign's birthday is officially celebrated every June by Trooping the Colour, a ceremony carried out on Horse Guards Parade by troops from the Household Division and watched by members of the royal family, invited guests and members of the public. The ceremony dates back to the early 18th century, when the flags (colours) of the battalion were carried (or "trooped") through the ranks to be saluted by the soldiers. Since 1748, this parade has also marked the Sovereign's official birthday and, since Edward VII's reign, the Sovereign has taken the salute in person. Until recently the Queen took the salute on horseback.

(above) Samuel Johnson published the first dictionary of the English language in 1755. Of the six clerks who helped him with the work, five were Scottish. His statue stands outside the Law Courts, on The Strand, near to where he lived.

(above right) A 13 foot high Queen Victoria looks along The Mall from the Queen Victoria Memorial, erected outside Buckingham Palace in 1911. The sculptor, Thomas Brock, was knighted at the unveiling ceremony.

(right) Oliver Cromwell stands, appropriately, outside the Houses of Parliament, where he served as Lord Protector from 1653 until his death in 1658.

There remain a multitude of examples of traditional dress to been seen all around the capital. The state opening of parliament involves The Gentleman Usher of the Black Rod, whose duties include carrying the mace in and out of the chamber of the House of Lords for the Lord Chancellor, whilst wearing a white wig and black knee-britches; the red-coated top-hatted doormen at the futuristic Lloyd's insurance building in the City are called waiters, recalling the beginnings of the insurance markets in a coffee-house. High court judges and barristers wear wigs and the pupils of Eton College wear top hats and tails.

Trafalgar Square is the setting for two winter traditions. Each December the people of Norway send a spruce tree to London in thanks for the support they received from Britain during World War II. The tree is erected in the square a week before Christmas and has been annually since 1947. The other more modern tradition associated with the square, but rather frowned upon these days, is that of revellers jumping into the fountains, however cold the weather, at midnight on December 31st, to celebrate the coming of the New Year. A similar disregard for personal comfort is shown by members of The Serpentine Swimming Club who have met in Hyde Park on every Christmas Day since 1864 to take part in the 100-yard "Peter Pan Cup" swimming race and who insist on taking a dip every Saturday morning of the year, even if it means breaking the ice first.

Trafalgar Square was completed in 1840 and the fountains, added in 1845, were replaced by Lutyens in 1939. In the background stands The National Gallery, built on the site of the former Whitehall Palace stables in 1838. The Christmas Tree is an annual gift from the people of Norway.

ALBERT

(left) The recently restored and re-gilded Albert Memorial was designed by George Gilbert Scott and erected over the two decades following Prince Albert's death from typhoid in 1861.

(above) The Coldstream Guards are one of the seven regiments making up the Household Division and are seen here in full dress uniform, on parade on the occasion of a State visit.

The Tower of London has stood sentinel at the south-eastern edge of old London for over 1,000 years. Building was started by William the Conqueror and it is seen here from the northern end of Tower Bridge.

(above) The City of London's Livery Companies were originally formed to protect the interests of individual crafts and trades. Some date back as far as the 12th century.

(above) Soldiers of the Household Cavalry leading their horses in the annual "musical ride", first performed in 1882.

(opposite page left) The name Big Ben was originally given to the 13-ton bell inside the tower. These days it is usually applied to the 320-foot tower itself. The minute-hands are 14 feet (4 metres) long and the pendulum weighs 650 lbs (300 kgs).

(above) The Household Cavalry, in common with the other six regiments of the Household Division, perform ceremonial duties as well as serving as regular professional soldiers. They are seen here entering the gates of Buckingham Palace.

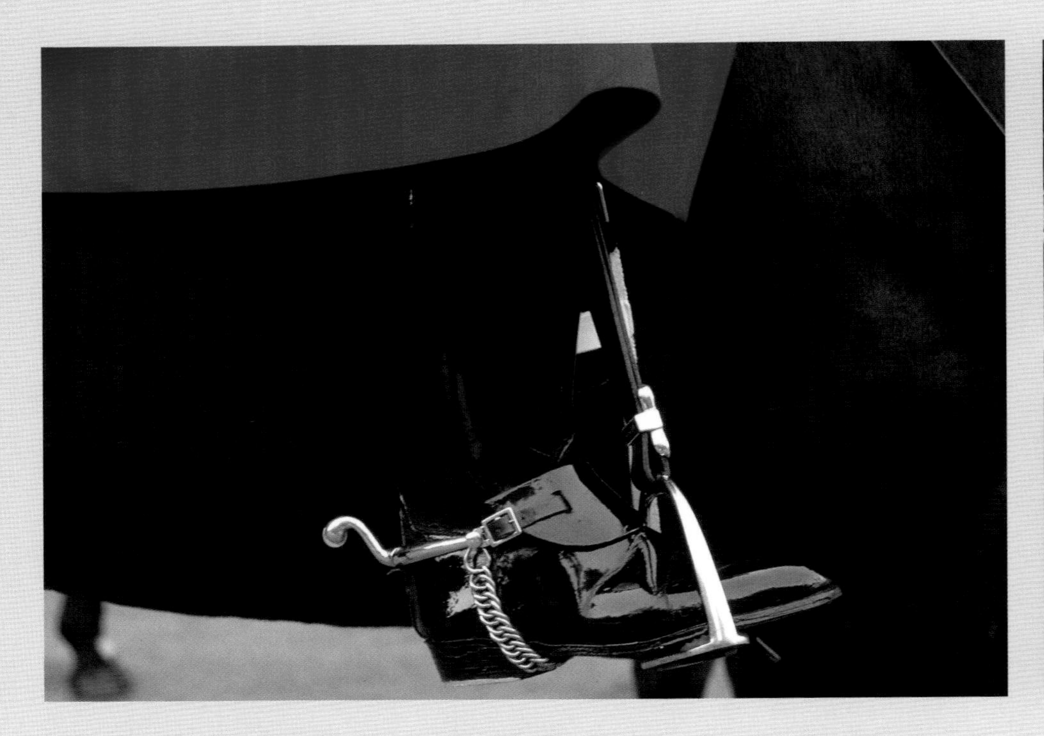

For ceremonial occasions every piece of a soldier's equipment must glisten and this guardsman sets a fine example.

The Royal Mews at Buckingham Palace houses over 100 coaches and carriages available for use on state occasions.

William III bought Kensington Palace in 1689 and had it extended by Christopher Wren. He lived there to escape the "pollution" of central London.

The modern buildings of the Sainsbury Wing of the National Gallery are seen here through the fountains in Trafalgar Square.

The Royal Hospital was founded in Chelsea by Charles II as a home for retired soldiers, known nowadays as Chelsea Pensioners.

The Royal Observatory was built at Greenwich in 1675. The zero degree line of longitude passes through this building.

Pomp and pageantry as Queen Elizabeth II and the Duke of Edinburgh, travelling in the Gold State Coach, are welcomed on the steps of St. Paul's Cathedral on the occasion of the Queen's jubilee celebrations.

The City of London

People in London do not go into "the city" they go "into town" or "up to town"; they go to the East End or the West End, north of the river or south of the river, or to the City. The City with a capital "C" is an institution as well as a place. Until the changes brought in by the introduction of electronic trading (the "big bang") in the 1980s, it was a well-defined place, the "square mile", with the Bank of England at its heart. Men (and it was almost always men) who were "something in the City" worked in the area which had been occupied by the Romans 2,000 years before, between The Tower in the east, London Wall in the north, the river in the south and St. Paul's in the west. In the electronic age bankers and brokers no longer need to be close enough to each other for messengers to carry details of their trades by hand from one firm to another on the same day, so offices are now spread around the capital, though still concentrated in "the square mile" and, a development of the late 20th century, the former docklands area of Canary Wharf on the Isle of Dogs.

The City (meaning financial services) is a massive contributor to the wealth of the United Kingdom. This is one of the largest world centres of banking, insurance, capital and commodity markets, shipping and of course the law firms and accountants to support them. The City has its own local government, The Corporation of London, with traditions dating back to its formation over 800 years ago, and its own Lord Mayor. Here too are the halls of the livery companies, the ancient guilds formed to protect and promote the interests of particular trades. Today they are little more than exclusive clubs, many of them great supporters of charities, but their names remind us of the time when the City was at the hub of London's commercial and trading life: Merchant Taylors, Fishmongers, Goldsmiths, Haberdashers, Ironmongers, Vintners and so on.

The predominantly wooden buildings of the area were substantially destroyed by the Great Fire of London in 1666. The fire is thought to have started in a baker's in Pudding Lane and the site is marked by a 202 foot (62 metre) Portland stone column known as The Monument. Designed by Wren and completed in 1671 it is the tallest free-standing stone column in the world. Inside, a spiral staircase with 311 steps leads to a platform with splendid views of the surrounding area. Something of the ancient street layout can be sensed from the top of The Monument for the area was rebuilt along the former street pattern after the fire, the only difference being that the houses could no longer be built of wood. It is only in the City that today's visitor can get a tangible sense of the layout of old London.

The Old Lady of Threadneedle Street, as The Bank of England is known, was established by William III in 1694. Despite its importance as the central bank it only passed into public ownership in 1946. This facade dates from the 1930s.

The names of the streets themselves are redolent of the past. Cheapside and Eastcheap incorporate the Norse word *chepe* from which we get the word shop, and were the sites of the great markets; there are Pudding Lane, Poultry, Threadneedle Street, Cornhill, Milk Street and Bread Street, all telling of the trade once followed in that particular area. Bishopsgate, Aldgate and Moorgate led to the gates in the city wall. Houndsditch, part of the original defensive moat was, according to John Stow, writing around 1600, full of "much filth, especially dead dogges".

At the heart of the City, literally and figuratively, is The Bank of England, known generally as just "The Bank". It is the UK's central bank and, as well as being responsible for issuing currency, it also advises the Treasury, sets interest rates and generally manages monetary policy. The Bank came into being by a royal charter of 1694 to help William III fund his war against France. It has been at its present location (whence its other nickname, "The Old Lady of Threadneedle Street") for

The griffin and the cross of St. George mark the formal boundaries of the City which, at 680 acres, covers a little over a square mile.

over 250 years but, apart from the outer wall, a remnant of Sir John Soane's design of around 1790, the present building was largely built in the 1930s.

Opposite the Bank, on the corner of Threadneedle Street and Cornhill, is The Royal Exchange, now a shopping centre so still, in a modest way, at the very heart of the City's commercial life. First opened as a meeting-place for traders and merchants in 1568 the present building, from 1844, is the third on the site. Across the road on the west side of this busy junction stands Mansion House, the official residence of The Lord Mayor. It was built between 1739 and 1752 on a site where the stocks once stood, in which criminals were clamped and pelted with old fruit and vegetables, or worse ...

Insurance broking and underwriting have been part of City life since the opening by Edward Lloyd of his coffee house in the 1680s. Here merchants and ships' captains would exchange information about vessels and cargoes and gradually the idea developed of bringing together groups of investors who would insure these vessels or cargoes against loss or damage. Lloyd's of London is perhaps the most recognisable name in insurance today and it still provides insurance cover through groups of individual underwriters, risking their own and their syndicate members' wealth. The old coffee house is long gone, yet the doormen in the present building are still known as "waiters". Insurance services, shipping, commodity trading and banking all grew together in this maze of bustling streets and alleys and are interdependent today as ever they were.

Just over from Lloyd's, in St. Mary Axe (a street named after a church which housed an axe said to have belonged to Attila the Hun) is the Baltic Exchange, the world's largest shipbroking marketplace. Here ships are bought and sold and chartered for voyages anywhere in the world. This too started life in a coffee house, The Virginia and Baltick, and until it was bombed out by the IRA in the early 1990's occupied the site where now stands the magnificent "Gherkin" tower. The Baltic moved into the building next door.

Yet another activity to have started its life in a coffee house is the London Stock Exchange. A building called the Stock Exchange was opened in Threadneedle Street in 1773 with an offshoot opening round the corner in Capel Court, off Old Broad Street in 1850. This is the site of the skyscraper where, until the advent of electronic trading and settlement in 1986, all the stockbrokers would meet to carry out their trades.

The Romans lived in what we know call the City for some 400 years. They were followed by the Saxons and in the 7th century King Ethelred of Kent not only instigated the building of the first St. Paul's but also introduced the system of rule through "peers" or aldermen advising and supporting the monarch. Close by the street called Aldermanbury, whose name is a continuing reminder of this system, stands the Guildhall, the centre of local government for at least 900 years. "Guild" comes from the same root as the German *Geld*, meaning money; this was possibly the place the Saxons came to pay their taxes. The present structure, off Gresham Street, was begun in 1411 but only the outer walls survived the fire of 1666, though it was rebuilt immediately afterwards. The biggest medieval crypts in

Somewhere in the North Sea there is an oil rig which looks like an office building ... Richard Rogers' 1980s Lloyd's of London building is not to everybody's taste. The doormen here are still known as "waiters", a reminder of Lloyd's beginnings as a coffee house.

The Royal Exchange, flanked by the Bank of England and Mansion House, was established on this site in 1565.

Leadenhall Market dates from 1445, having started in the nearby gardens of the Neville family's lead-roofed mansion.

The winding, medieval City streets are, not surprisingly with such wealthy tenants, home to London's best modern architecture.

London are below Guildhall and excavations in 1988 revealed the remains of a Roman amphitheatre below Guildhall Yard.

The City occupies about 680 acres (slightly more than 1 square mile) and contains the UK's most concentrated wealth of ecclesiastical architecture (described in more detail in the next chapter). The visitor can still see Saxon, Norman and medieval remains and hear the sound of Bow Bells and many of the other peals celebrated in *Oranges and Lemons,* but the area is best-known for its 23 Wren Churches, built in the aftermath of the Great Fire of London. These are dotted all around the City, built on the sites of the buildings destroyed by the fire. St. Paul's itself is of course Wren's enduring monument. Built over 35 years, completed in 1710 and restored and cleaned in the early 21st century, it is a magnificent testimonial to one man's artistic genius.

Since the development of electronic technology employment patterns in the City have changed significantly. In the 1970s over 700,000 people undertook the daily commute to the square mile; today the number is little over half of that. The location which has benefited most significantly from these changes is The Isle of Dogs in London's old docklands, downriver from Tower Bridge. Here in 1987, due to the government's desire to revitalize the area, plus the vision of the Canadian Reichman brothers, the building of Canary Wharf was commenced. The initial 850 foot (260 metre) tower with its own shops, restaurants and railway station was the catalyst for the regeneration of the whole area into what is, in effect, a second City, served by a greatly improved infrastructure, including the Docklands Light Railway and the Jubilee tube line. The huge dock basins have been preserved with many of the new buildings beside the water or very close by, so that Canary Wharf and the surrounding area provide a complete architectural contrast with the narrow, winding, medieval street plan of the City. The area may lack the sheer historical intensity of its neighbour to the west but the architecture is stunning and a visit to Docklands can be combined with a trip to the Maritime Museum and Royal Observatory at Greenwich, accessible via a little-known Victorian pedestrian tunnel running under the river between the Isle of Dogs and the restored clipper-ship, *Cutty Sark*.

Few commute to the City or to Docklands by car; it has become increasingly difficult since many City streets were closed to through traffic as part of the construction of "the ring of steel" in the 1980s to try to give some protection against further IRA bombings. Several Thames-taxi or river-bus services have been tried over the years but each seems to have failed to attract sufficient support to remain viable. The area is however well-served by buses and the tube and the City even has its own underground, The Waterloo and City Line, known to all as "The Drain". It is London's second-oldest underground line, running only between Waterloo and Bank. It has a reputation as London's politest line with commuters forming orderly queues at both stations.

City commuters may be (relatively) polite but they are no longer as instantly recogniseable as they were only 30 or 40 years ago when any self-respecting City gent would wear a pin-striped suit, a bowler hat and be carrying a rolled umbrella and a copy of the Financial Times. And *always* black lace-up shoes.

An intriguing set of traffic lights in the "second City", the Isle of Dogs. Since 1987 this area has attracted around one third of the workers formerly based in the square mile.

(above) At the western edge of the City and beyond the city walls is Smithfield meat market, which was already established here in the 12th century. This view towards St. Paul's takes in the dormer windows in the roof of the 19th century market hall.

(next page left) The early-morning view from the Southwark river-bank over the barges shows the pride of place of St. Paul's in the London skyline, alongside the 275-years younger Tower 42 (formerly NatWest Tower) to the east.

(next page right) London's Docklands have been turned over from wool and coal to mammon. The building of these late 20th / early 21st century skyscrapers at Canary Wharf has encouraged the departure of many firms from their traditional home, the City.

HSBC
DOCKLAND
SCOUT PROJECT

Canary Wharf has its own station on the Docklands Light Railway system. The improvement in public transport links has been central to the regeneration of Docklands.

Victorian terraces of London stock brick nestle in the shadow of the Broadgate development, near Liverpool Street station. The complex includes an outdoor ice-skating rink.

On the site of the old Baltic Exchange and towering over the 14th century St. Andrew's Undershaft stands one of the City's most adventurous buildings, affectionately known as "The Gherkin".

The entrance to the Lloyd's of London building off Leadenhall Street. The business had its origins in Edward Lloyd's coffee house, popular in the 17th century with ships' captains and sailors.

(left) Modest Edwardian terraced houses in the foreground and behind them the 850 foot tower of Canary Wharf. This first tower, designed by Cesar Pelli and I.M. Pei, was completed in the early 1990s, with over four million square feet of office space.

(above) Seen through one of the suspension spans of Tower Bridge, Tower 42 rises above its neighbours to a height of 600 feet. Formerly the NatWest Tower, the bank moved out after the building was damaged by an IRA bomb.

(above) Well-paid City workers support a wealth of good food stores and restaurants.

(right) No. 1 London Bridge represented the City's first real move south of the river.

Two hundred years separate the old and the new on the Isle of Dogs

Domine nos dirige - "God be our guide" - the motto of the City Corporation

The "Gherkin", designed by Foster & Partners, offers evidence of the dynamism and constant self-renewal of the City, home to London's most innovative architecture.

London and the Church

The present-day St. Paul's Cathedral, seat of the Bishop of London, is the fifth religious building to have occupied the site. Christopher Wren had been asked as early as 1663 to draw up plans for a major refurbishment of the old St. Paul's but only began work on the new building some 9 years after the Great Fire of 1666 had destroyed the existing church and he finished the task 35 years later, in 1710. In contrast to Westminster Abbey, a building which evolved over hundreds of years, St. Paul's is the work of one man's genius and has remained relatively unchanged for some 300 years.

Westminster Abbey is, by contrast, a fascinating architectural hotch-potch and of immense interest to any student of England's history over the first half of the last millennium. Westminster was originally a monastery, hence Westminster Abbey, not to be confused with the Roman Catholic Westminster Cathedral, built between 1896 and 1903. William the Conqueror had himself crowned King at Westminster Abbey on Christmas Day 1066 but the present structure was begun under the reign of Henry III in 1245 and completed in 1532. The 103 feet (31 metre) nave is the highest in England and the interior is packed with funerary monuments ranging from the reclining marble statues of monarchs and politicians, to the famous poets' corner. Right next to the Abbey is St. Margaret's Westminster, the parish church of the House of Commons. It was last rebuilt in 1486 and Winston Churchill was married there in 1908.

Today within the City boundaries there are some 55 churches, a cathedral and a synagogue, together exemplifying practically every major phase of English architectural history. There are fragments of Roman and Saxon building to be seen in All Hallows (near the Tower of London) and St. Bride's (in Fleet Street). It is thought that St. Bride's stands on the site of London's first church, dedicated to St. Bridget and built in the 6th century. St. Bride's 18th century spire has been the inspiration for multi-tiered wedding cakes since it was first imitated by a local pastry-cook in the late 1700s.

The crypt of St. Mary le Bow in Cheapside dates back to 1090 (a cockney is defined as someone born within the sound of Bow Bells), whilst St. Bartholomew's, near Smithfield market, was founded in 1123 and can claim to be the oldest surviving parish church in London. The Temple Church, within the barristers' Middle and Inner Temple complex of buildings, between Fleet Street and the river, was consecrated in 1185 and has one of only five surviving circular naves in England. This was the church of the Knights Templar and an effigy in stone of Sir Robert de Ros, who died in 1227, survives there intact.

St. Martin-in-the-Fields, overlooking Trafalgar Square, has been a sanctuary for the homeless since its crypt was opened to offer shelter to soldiers returning from the First World War. There has been a church on this site for almost 800 years.

At the time of the Great Fire the City had 108 churches and 87 of them were destroyed or badly damaged. Of these 51 were rebuilt with funds raised from a tax on coal passing through the City by boat. Work was overseen by Christopher Wren, whose assistants included Nicholas Hawksmoor. Of the surviving churches, 23 (excluding St. Paul's) are the work of Wren. They display a surprising architectural variety and house amongst them England's most concentrated collection of fine woodcarving, some of which is also to be seen in the Spanish and Portuguese Synagogue. This was built for Sephardic Jews between 1699 and 1701 and is the oldest surviving English synagogue. Although Jews had been permitted to settle in England by the mid 17th century (for the first time since 1290) they were still not allowed to build synagogues on "the high street", so this building is tucked away in a rather anonymous courtyard off Bevis Marks.

Many of the City churches offer an insight into London's secular history as well as its religious past. St. Andrew Undershaft, in Leadenhall Street, first mentioned in records dating back to 1147, is so-called because its steeple was overshadowed each year by a huge maypole (a "shaft") erected for the May Day celbrations. These revelries were finally banned in 1517 because of the riotous behaviour of young apprentices, the "football hooligans" of their day. There is a statue in this church of London's first historian, John Stow (died 1605) holding a real quill pen in his hand. In an annual ceremony the Lord Mayor of London still gives the pen to the schoolboy deemed most worthy of it, and replaces the statue's quill with a new one. St. Olave's (Hart Street) is the only survivor of five churches once dedicated to King Olaf of Norway, who sided with Ethelred, King of England, against Viking invaders in 1014. Parish records show that a "Mother Goose" was buried there, as was Mary Ramsay, who is believed to have introduced the plague to London in 1664.

Amongst more modern treasures in the Square Mile St. Stephen's (Walbrook), thought by many to be Wren's masterpiece, has a 1980s altarpiece by Henry Moore. St. Michael's (Cornhill) has some excellent Victorian stained glass but perhaps the most impressive stained glass can be seen just on the fringes of the City at St. Ethelreda's, off Holborn in Ely Place, former London home of the bishops of Ely. This church became the first to revert to Catholicism after the Reformation, some 3 centuries earlier and has massive matching east and west stained glass windows.

On the south side of the Thames, by Lambeth Bridge, is London's finest example of medieval domestic building, Lambeth Palace. In common with many London buildings it shows the architecture of several periods, from the undercroft of 1207, to the 15th century red-brick gatehouse and the 19th century crenellations. Whilst not itself a place of worship, it serves as the London residence of the Archbishop of Canterbury and the complex incudes a chapel. The garden is believed to be the oldest in London and only that of Buckingham Palace is bigger.

Each part of London has its own examples of places of worship, many of them local parish churches of greater or lesser architectural merit, some of them very grand indeed. London's prime Roman Catholic church, after Westminster Cathedral, is the 19th century Italianate-baroque Brompton Oratory, located between Harrods and the Victoria and Albert Museum. Also outside the boundaries of the City is South-

In the year 601 Pope Gregory nominated London as Britain's principal bishopric and three years later the cathedral church of St. Paul's was built. The present Wren church is the fifth to occupy this dominant site.

William the Conqueror was crowned at Westminster Abbey on Christmas Day 1066 and since the 1300s all English monarchs have been crowned here on the oak Coronation Chair made by Master Walter of Durham.

wark Cathedral (by London Bridge), originally an Augustinian priory. It was built on the site of a Roman villa, some of whose mosaic tiles can still be seen in the floor of the present building. Construction began in the early 1200s but it was substantially rebuilt in the subsequent two centuries. Trafalgar Square boasts St. Martin-in-the-Fields. When the first chapel was built here in 1222 it really was surrounded by fields. The present building, dating from 1772-6 was erected to serve the newly-fashionable area of Covent Garden. This church has a long tradition of helping the homeless and holds regular lunchtime concerts of classical music.

St. James's (Piccadilly), the only Wren church to be built on a new site, very close to Piccadilly Circus, was consecrated in 1684. It has a marble font carved by Grinling Gibbons. The church was badly damaged by bombing and the old graveyard has been turned into a garden of remembrance to commemorate the courage of Londoners during the 1940's air raids. It is a refreshing haven in that busy part of town.

The "other" St. Paul's, in Covent Garden, was designed by Inigo Jones, architect of much of the area, including the piazza, and completed in 1633. It was the first Anglican church to be built on a new site in London since the Reformation which had occurred 100 years earlier. This is "the actors' church" and although the main entrance appears to be onto the piazza it is actually in the courtyard at the back of the building.

St. John's (Clerkenwell) is on the site of the 11th century Priory of St. John of Jerusalem which was the London "home" of the Knights of Malta, or Knights

The main part of Westminster Abbey was built between 1245 and 1532 in the French Gothic style. The familiar towers shown opposite are an 18th century addition.

Hospitaller. At the dissolution of the monasteries in 1536-41 the church was given to Henry VIII who used it to store his hunting tents. He will have hunted on land formerly owned by the Knights, land which gave its name to the later London suburb of St. John's Wood.

Immigrants have always made their mark on London's religious architecture. Despite having lived and worked here for hundreds of years, not always officially tolerated, the Jews built their first synagogue at the turn of the 17th and 18th centuries. Greek orthodox immigrants were granted the right to build their first London church, in Soho, in 1677, but within 10 years it was confiscated by the authorities for no apparent reason and handed over to the Huguenot immigrants, who had themselves fled religious persecution in France. Greek immigration increased significantly in the early 19th century and led in 1877 to the building of the magnificent Church of the Divine Wisdom (St. Sophia) in Moscow Road.

The cathedral of the Russian orthodox church in London is in Kensington's Ennismore Gardens. The parish was founded in 1741 to serve the Russian embassy but moved to the present building, formerly the Anglican church of All Saints, in 1956. It is a Victorian building housing a large collection of icons, many of which were salvaged from the Russian embassy at the time of the 1917 revolution.

The immigration patterns of the latter part of the 20th century have led to the building of hundreds of mosques and London is now thought to have more mosques than any city west of Istanbul. Britain's oldest surviving mosque was completed in the late 19th century and is in Woking in Surrey. Although a handful survive from the early 20th century, the majority of London mosques are the product of late 20th century immigration and can be found dotted around the whole of the city, often standing out in the uniformity of suburbia through their uncompromisingly oriental architectural styles.

Wimbledon is home not only to the tennis championships but also to Wat Buddhapadipa, the first Buddhist temple to be built in the United Kingdom, in 1976. It is a visually-stunning Thai-styled building, designed for monastic use, and the only one of its kind in Europe. The most significant new religious building of the last decade is, however, the enormous Shri Swaminarayan Hindu Temple in north London's Neasden suburb, a quite magnificently decorated exotic giant of a building in an otherwise fairly unprepossessing part of town. The temple is named after the 18th century guru, Lord Swaminarayan, who walked the length of India barefoot, preaching the values of social care for the poor. This massive edifice took only three years from concept to consecration and was built with the use of 2000 tons of Italian marble and nearly 3000 tons of Bulgarian limestone, all of which was first shipped to India, to be shaped by more than 1,000 skilled craftsmen - all volunteers - then individually numbered and sent to London to be pieced together in situ.

The church of St. Mary le Strand dominates the road which has always been a main artery on the western side of the city and in Saxon times was at its very heart. The building of the present church was started in 1711.

(above) The west face of St. Paul's looks down Ludgate Hill where, according to legend, King Lud built a gate to the city in 66BC.

(left) The two-storey portico forming the main entrance to St. Paul's was completed to Christopher Wren's design in 1710.

(right) James Thornhill's decorations in the 220-feet high baroque dome feature scenes from the life of St. Paul.

(left) The astonishing Shri Swaminarayan Hindu temple was built in the north London suburb of Neasden in only 3 years. It is dedicated to the guru, Lord Swaminarayan, who walked the length of India barefoot, preaching the value of care for the poor.

(above) Nicholas Hawksmoor was employed by Christopher Wren as a clerk at the age of 18. He left his mark on many London buildings, including Greenwich Hospital, Kensington Palace and Christ Church, Spitalfields, seen here from the Spitalfields market, and consecrated in 1729.

(next page left) Bunhill Fields cemetery in the City was, from the mid 17th to the mid 18th century, London's main burial ground for non-conformists. "Bunhill" may be a corrupt form of "bone hill".

THE REMAINS OF

Tombs and monuments in the old part of Highgate Cemetery.

Fallen gravestones are gathered together in a churchyard in St. Pancras.

Southwark Cathedral was elevated to cathedral status only in the 19th century but there have been churches on this site, near London Bridge, for over 1400 years. John Harvard, founder of the eponymous American university, was baptised here in 1607.

Government and Law

The Palace of Westminster (Houses of Parliament), rebuilt after fire destroyed the previous building in 1834, has been the home of British government for almost a thousand years.

The government of the nation at the current location dates from the reign of Edward the Confessor. Just prior to the Norman invasion in the middle of the 11th century he built the first Palace of Westminster on the north bank of the Thames and so provided an alternative location for the government to that within the old city walls. It remained the focal point of English government through 25 monarchs until Henry VIII moved his court downriver to Greenwich in 1529, a move reversed by his successors. Despite the recent devolution of substantial powers to the governments of Scotland and Wales and, to a lesser extent, Northern Ireland, London is still at the heart of the legislature for the United Kingdom. It is also home to the Lord Mayor of London, the elected mayor and the Greater London Authority, the local government of the metropolis itself.

Westminster became the home of the *curia regis* or "king's court", an early combination of a council of ministers and a law court: in other words, a body concerned with both the creation and administration of laws. This was the institution from which the higher courts of law and the privy council have since evolved. It was, at first, a general advisory body for the king, comprising the most important and powerful feudal lords. This small group developed into a council (or group of advisors – counsellors) with specific committees, formed to assist the king in his judicial work. In 1178 Henry II appointed five members of the *curia regis* to form a special court of justice required to remain in one place regardless of where the king's travels might take him. This was the beginning of the separation of the judiciary from the legislature. About the time of Edward I certain duties of the *curia regis* were devolved to the king's secret advisory group, the later "privy council" from which came the modern idea of a "cabinet" of senior ministers.

Affairs of state are debated in the chambers of the House of Commons and the House of Lords within the Palace of Westminster, more colloquially known as The Houses of Parliament. The familiar building was commissioned in 1837 after a fire had destroyed all of the previous one, save for the medieval Great Hall, now part of the House of Lords, and the Jewel Tower, across the road from the present buildings. There were 97 plans submitted to the architectural competition for the new buildings and the winners were Charles Barry and Augustus Pugin, the latter being best known for the lavish decoration of the interior of the buildings. The House of Lords was able to sit by 1847, the Commons by 1851, but it was 1860 before the clock-tower of Big Ben was finished. A light shining from the tower at night indicates that parliament is sitting. The relatively few visitors allowed into the buildings are always amused to find that, as they pass through that area where the Commons give way to the Lords, the carpeting and the upholstery of the furniture changes from green to red.

Britain does not have a written constitution. Parliament, with its 651 elected Members of Parliament, may legislate as it pleases, subject to Britain's obligations as a member of the European Union. It can make or change any law and can overturn established conventions or turn them into law. The validity of an Act of Parliament, once passed, cannot be disputed in the law courts, only interpreted. In the early 1990s there were almost 1200 members of the House of Lords, over half of them hereditary peers who had inherited their titles and their right to play a part

(next page) The clock tower of Big Ben, completed in 1860, rises to 320 feet at the eastern end of The Palace of Westminster. The first bell developed a crack after only a few months and a smaller hammer had to be fitted.

in Britain's government. In recent years a fundamental overhaul of the Lords has meant the almost complete removal of hereditary peers from this role and their replacement mainly by appointees of the main political parties.

British governments are advised by civil servants who are required to be apolitical and to assist in the execution of policy decided by the government of the day. Unlike the US system, where civil servants are appointed by an incoming administration, the British Civil Service is a permanent cadre of professionals chosen at the higher levels by competitive examinations, first established as early as 1855 (the Chinese had had the same idea in the Han Dynasty, which started in 206 BC). Many of the great departments of government, including the Treasury, the Foreign Office and the Ministry of Defence (or, in other times, the War Office), together with their ministers and civil servants, have their headquarters in the street which runs from the Palace of Westminster to Trafalgar Square - Whitehall. It takes its name from Henry VIII's Whitehall Palace which stood on the banks of the Thames, just south of the present-day Trafalgar Square. All that remains of the palace today is the Inigo Jones Banqueting House, commissioned by James I and opened in 1622. The name "Whitehall" has become synonymous with the administration of government, though nowadays an increasing number of government and civil service departments are being moved away from London.

In the middle ages the city had begun to grow, and as the mayor and aldermen had no jurisdiction outside the original Roman boundaries, local matters beyond the walls came to be managed by parish councils, manorial courts or justices of the peace (magistrates). In the 19th century a few pan-London authorities did come into being – the Metropolitan Police, the London School Board, and the London County Council – but it was not until 1965 that the suburban sprawl of London was redefined as Greater London and brought under the centralised control of the Greater London Council, or GLC. In 1986 the GLC was abolished by the Thatcher government and power was again returned to local authorities. Following a referendum the new Greater London Authority was established in 2000 to attempt once again to centralise many of the functions of London's government. Under the GLA London has, for the first time ever, a directly-elected mayor (not to be confused with the City's Lord Mayor) with real executive power. The Lord Mayor of London is actually the leader of the Corporation of London, the local authority for the City (see earlier chapter). The title dates back to at least 1189 and over 700 men and one woman have held the post to date. Nowadays the position is largely ambassadorial for the business interests of the "square mile".

The GLC met in the Portland stone County Hall on the south side of Westminster Bridge and adjacent to the current site of the London Eye. The GLA is also housed by the river but in very different style: City Hall is a Norman Foster-designed building, opened in 2002 on the south side of the river near Tower Bridge. Ten storeys high, it is energy-efficient and is like nothing else in London, a sort of leaning glass bulb looking like a soft-boiled egg on the point of toppling over.

Governments make laws and the judges interpret them; that the two institutions have grown side by side in the capital city is no surprise. The two highest courts outside of the House of Lords and the European Court are the Central Criminal Court, known universally by the street where it is located, Old Bailey, and the Royal Courts of Justice in the Strand. As its full name suggests Old Bailey is where the most important and complex criminal cases are heard. There has been a court on the site since 1539 and the location was chosen to be adjacent to Newgate prison. The present building was completed in 1907 and is famous for its rooftop statue of Justice, holding a set of scales in one hand and a sword in the other. The Royal Courts of Justice constitute the principal English courts dealing with civil cases such as property issues (the Court of Chancery) and that wide range of cases which can be settled by the payment of damages. These are heard in the Queen's (or "King's") Bench division, the name being a reminder of those first "law lords" required by Henry II to stay put at Westminster, on their bench, while the king was travelling.

The Central Criminal Court is known by the name of the street in which it has sat since 1539, Old Bailey. The present building, with the familiar statue of Justice, scales in one hand and a sword in the other, was completed in 1907.

This Victorian statue of King Richard I, the Lionheart, at the Palace of Westminster is by Carlo Marochetti, RA. Richard was crowned in 1189 and spent only one year of his life in England. He never learned to speak English.

(above) The Guildhall has been at the heart of City governance for at least 900 years and is built on the site of a Roman amphitheatre. The present building was begun in 1411 but badly damaged in the Great Fire of 1666 and again in World War II.

(right) The Victorian-gothic Law Courts, with over 1,000 rooms, have their familiar entrance on The Strand. The slums of this area were cleared in 1871 to make way for the building of the courthouse, which finally opened in 1882.

The grand Victorian-gothic building was opened in 1882 and is today generally referred to simply as the Law Courts.

The English judicial system differentiates between solicitors, who are instructed directly by their clients and who may represent them in lower courts, and barristers, who are instructed by solicitors and who are admitted to higher courts to fulfill the role of advocate. The barristers are the ones who wear powdered wigs and black gowns when appearing before the judge in court. To be "admitted to the bar" is an arcane and traditional process which had its origins in the royal summons to act as an advocate. These days the trainee must be accepted into an internship or "pupillage" with a qualified barrister. He must also pass the appropriate examinations and be admitted to membership of one of the four ancient Inns of Court. The Inns of Court have for centuries had a special place in the English legal structure. Formed in the 14th, 15th and 16th centuries these institutions have the sole right to admit law students as barristers. Called Inns because they originally provided accommodation for pupils and teachers, they now accommodate the offices or "chambers" of many of the barristers. As part of the process of qualifying trainee barristers have to attend 12 dinners at their Inn. The origins of this date from the time when qualified practitioners dined with the students who picked up part of their education from their fellow diners and from readings given by a senior member of the Inn (the Master Reader) after the meal. Even today, at least at

Middle Temple, the students are required to be present both at the commencement of the formal meal and at the grace that completes it.

Lincoln's Inn, the oldest of the four Inns, takes its name from the Earl of Lincoln, who died in 1311, and it occupies over 11 acres next to Lincoln's Inn Fields, London's largest open square. A tablet on the outside of the north wall of the Old Hall in Lincoln's Inn records that the hall was built "in the fifth year of King Henry VII", so it was there before Christopher Columbus set sail for the Americas. Gray's Inn, founded in 1569, is the newest of the four. Shakespeare's *A Comedy of Errors* was first performed in Gray's Inn Hall in 1594 and Charles Dickens was once employed here as a clerk. The hall's 16th century screen is believed to have been made from the wood of a galley from the Spanish Armada. In the grounds of Middle and Inner Temple stands the Temple Church, built by the Knights Templar in the middle of the 12th century. When the order was abolished in 1312 lawyers moved in to the property and formed two Inns of Court, the Inner and Middle Temples. The 17th century buildings of the former offices of the "King's Bench" stand within Inner Temple, in King's Bench Walk.

Staple Inn overlooking High Holborn is sometimes mistakenly described as an Inn of Court but was actully an Inn of Chancery, also a medieval school for lawyers. The façade dates from 1586 and although it has seen much restoration and alteration it remains one of London's few surviving Tudor buildings.

A small number of senior barristers go on to become judges, whose role ultimately is to interpret common law, essentially the decisions, or precedents of earlier judges and administer the laws passed by Parliament. They must also guide juries in their assessment of the facts, and pass appropriate sentences. Judges wear red robes and a wig in court but the long horsehair wigs are generally only for ceremonial occasions; in court a short wig is worn by barristers and judges alike.

(right) Somerset House, which today houses the Courtauld Institute of Art and its galleries, is built on the site of the medieval residences of the Bishops of Chester and Worcester. These were replaced in 1550 by the palace of the Duke of Somerset, after whom the present building of 1786 is named.

(next page left) The Tower of London was started by William the Conqueror, by then William I, in 1078 and finished 200 years later. Its main purpose was unquestionably defence.

(next page right) From the London Eye the curved façade of County Hall looks more like Vienna than London. Opened in 1922 it housed the offices of the Greater London Council until its abolition under the Thatcher government in 1986.

ENTRY TO THE TRAITORS' GATE

OUNTY HALL
SAATCHI GALLERY
SAATCHI GALLERY

The offices of the Greater London Authority, established in 1999, occupy a site once at the heart of London's "lewd entertainments" in Southwark, on the southern bank of the Thames.

The statue of Sir Winston Churchill, by Ivor Roberts-Jones, was unveiled in Parliament Square in 1973. At the time it caused controversy with one newspaper complaining that the artist had made Churchill look "more like Mussolini".

Staple Inn, whose shady courtyard above is just off High Holborn, served as a school for lawyers from 1378 to 1884. It was one of nine so-called Inns of Chancery, whose original function was to train the clerks who prepared writs for the English courts.

The timber-framed façade of Staple Inn is one of the very few surviving examples of Tudor architecture in London. It was built in 1586. Most of the other buildings of this period were lost to the Great Fire of London or to property developers in the 19th and 20th centuries.

Protestors outside the Palace of Westminster and thus in clear view of members of parliament entering and leaving the building. This particular group has occupied the same place for several years.

Living in London

London is often described as a collection of villages. Originally settled in the area now known as the City, London grew to absorb the neighbouring areas of Holborn, Southwark, Clerkenwell, Rotherhithe and Greenwich, and later the villages of Chelsea and Fulham, Hampstead and Highgate, and many more. Little of what we see in London today is the result of any architectural grand plan and much of its residential property development occurred through speculative building rather than centralised planning. In the 17th, 18th and 19th centuries a small number of landowners developed huge greenfield sites around London for housing. Sir Thomas Grosvenor's bride brought him the whole of what is now Mayfair as her dowry.

London is divided into dozens of postal districts and to a Londoner the post-code is a clue to more than location: it "says something about you". At one period or another in the past 50 years Londoners would have associated SW7 (Chelsea) with artists, pop stars and fashion models, W1 (Mayfair) with inherited wealth and property developers, NW3 (Hampstead) with writers and intellectuals and SW4 (Clapham) with aspiring young professionals. Amongst those who live all or most of their lives in London there is often a strong loyalty to one part of town rather than another and few people make the move from north of the river to south, or vice versa. A Londoner likes to feel part of his own village.

The visitor to London who manages to get beyond the West End, if only to museum-land (South Kensington), never fails to be struck by an almost unique aspect of London housing: the terraces (or as the Americans say, "row houses"). In England the first streets of houses with uniform fronts were built by the Huguenot entrepreneur Nicholas Barbon in the rebuilding after the Great Fire of London, although Paris had actually been first with the Place des Vosges (1605 –1612). Many of the elegant terraces of London, in Belgravia, Chelsea, Kensington and so on, were built by property speculators of the 18th and 19th centuries, the most celebrated of whom was Thomas Cubitt (1788 -1855). The son of a Norfolk farmer, he learned his trade as a ship's carpenter. He was a builder rather than a landowner and opened his own firm in Gray's Inn Road, becoming the first builder to have the modern system of employing tradesmen on permanent wages, instead of finding different freelance contractors for each job. Cubitt was responsible for an astonishing amount of what we consider to be typical London housing. He worked on speculative developments in Camden Town and Islington, parts of St. Pancras, including Gordon Square and Tavistock Square, where work began in 1820 for a group of landowners including the Duke of Bedford. Cubitt was commissioned in 1824 by Richard Grosvenor, the 2nd Marquess of Westminster, to create a great swathe of buildings in Belgravia, centred on Belgrave Square, and also in Pimlico. On top of all this he was responsible for the north and west sides of Eaton Square, much of Bloomsbury, and the eastern face of Buckingham Palace. He also built and personally financed over half a mile of the Thames Embankment. This pattern of building houses to a fairly standard plan and selling them once completed has characterised UK property development ever since and the terrace, an efficient way of using limited space, has retained its popularity.

The elegant mansions of Holland Park stand on land named after the Earl of Holland, whose family inherited the estate in the 1620s. The present houses were built in the second half of the 19th century.

Perhaps because of their love of gardening, the English like to live in houses rather than flats, but like any other city where land is expensive, London has its share of multiple-occupant dwellings. Until the 1960s there was a law limiting the height of buildings in London. Its repeal led to office skyscrapers but few residential ones. A significant exception is the Barbican Estate whose huge towers have dominated the City skyline since the 1970s though there are many examples left of municipal housing from the sixties and seventies, especially in the East End and the suburbs. The young Londoner of today is likely to start his independent life in a

White or cream-stuccoed terraces, often converted to flats, are typical of many parts of west and south-west London.

Fournier Street, a fine example of early Georgian terraced housing, whose street signs today are in Bengali as well as English.

rented flat, perhaps shared with friends, buying his first flat or house in his early thirties.

Londoners have learned to love their river. Fifty years ago the metropolitan Thames was still lined with dingy, dilapidated warehouses, wharves and docks. Since the closure of the docks and the loss of river-borne trade, there has been a gradual realisation that the river is really a rather attractive place to work and to live. Today the waterfront bustles with modern offices and apartments and tasteful warehouse conversions. There is even a 44-mile footpath, most of which runs alongside the river, from Hampton Court in the west to Dartford in the east.

Immigration has always affected the character of different parts of London. Over the past few centuries there have been the Huguenots from France, lascar sailors from India, freed African and Caribbean slaves; in the thirties the tens of thousands of mainly German and Austrian Jews fleeing Hitler, and in the fifties the great optimistic waves of immigrants from the colonies, particularly the West Indies. The latter half of the 20th century brought Ugandan Asians, evicted by Idi Amin, Vietnamese and Chinese, refugees from the Balkan States and from war-torn Africa. Finally the liberal labour laws of the EU have opened Britain's borders to workers from most of the rest of the continent. Within Britain London has attracted by far the highest proportion of all of these groups and each has in some way or another made its mark on the capital.

In the 19th century thousands of Italians fled political instability at home, and by 1900 there were 10,000 in London - a very sizable community at that time. They gravitated to Clerkenwell and many of them were builders. The area around St. Peter's church in Clerkenwell is still home to many Italian cafes and food shops. Thousands of southern Italians arrived in London in the 1950s and 1960s and many settled in Soho - then a cheap and rather seedy part of town – and started to work in and then become owners of cafes and restaurants. They made a huge impact on a generation of Londoners for whom spaghetti and frothy coffee were intriguing and unfamiliar delicacies. From this Italian-driven scene as much as anything else grew the idea of London as a stylish, cosmopolitan and, eventually, swinging city. Soho too was able to re-invent itself, firstly as the centre of London's illicit sex industry, and subsequently as a sophisticated leisure district and home to the UK's burgeoning media industry.

The Huguenot silk-weavers' houses still stand in Fournier Street in Spitalfields but the street signs are now in Bengali as well as in English and in neighbouring Brick Lane colourful silks and the smell of curry mark the character of the area in the new millennium. No immigrant community has so completely made its mark on one London borough as the Bangladeshis (or Bengalis) have on Tower Hamlets. More than one in three Tower Hamlets residents now consider themselves to be ethnic Bangladeshis. In Spitalfields, including Brick Lane, they make up just under 60% of the population. It is a rapidly growing community too. In 1991, there were about 37,000 Bangladeshis in Tower Hamlets, and very few anywhere else in London but by 2001 the population exceeded 67,000 in Tower Hamlets and large new communities had become established in West Ham and King's Cross. The Bangladeshi

Muslims who came to Britain in the 1970s were poorer, and often less educated, than the Indian Hindus who preceded them, but they quickly developed one good idea into a national institution. There had been "Indian" restaurants before but the Bengalis opened more and more with astonishing energy and enthusiasm. The speed with which exotic novelties such as mango chutney and rogan josh were absorbed into the British culinary mainstream is quite remarkable and no part of London today is without its curry house. In the early part of the 21st century it is said that the Briton's favourite food is chicken tikka masala, a curry dish invented by Bengali immigrants to suit the UK palate.

Stockwell, a relatively poor area of south London became for some reason the chosen destination for a wave of Portuguese immigration in the 1970s and 80s. Many of them took jobs as domestic servants but a few Portuguese started to open restaurants on South Lambeth Road, encouraged by the local authorities, who were pleased to see respectable businesses challenging the area's drug economy. London now has numerous Portuguese restaurants and some 27,000 Portuguese live in Stockwell - the largest community outside Portugal itself.

Clothing factories brought hundreds of Vietnamese refugees into Hackney in the early 1980s, but when their jobs went overseas in the mid-1990s (often back to Vietnam) the textile workers were forced to find a new trade. A few entrepreneurs had been to visit the US, saw the ubiquitous "nail parlours" and realised there were none in Britain. In less than 10 years, having started with no training or experience, a handful of Vietnamese have learned the trade and today this small immigrant group, only 15-20,000 in total, own more than 300 nail parlours in London alone. As ever they have also brought their own distinctive cuisine with them.

A complete book could be written on the immigrant groups in London's melting pot. Soho boasts its own "Chinatown", and Earls Court Road is known as "Kangaroo Valley". There are Japanese in Ealing and Acton and wealthy Russians are moving into Mayfair and Belgravia. Temporary immigrants, frequently attracted by high-paying jobs in the City include Americans, who gravitate to Chelsea and Holland Park, French who choose South Kensington, to be close to the French Lycée and Scandinavians who aim for the south-western suburbs, where there is a popular Swedish school. The presence of all of them has helped to create a cosmopolitan city matched for its variety of cultures by few other places in the world.

Once a row of humble workers' cottages, these are now highly desirable commuter homes overlooking Wimbledon Common.

Wrought-iron railings were often melted down to assist the war effort in the 1940s. These survivors are in Bedford Square.

(next page left) A typical iron pillar box.

(next page right) The elegant facade of Bedford Square laid out by William Scott and Thomas Crewer from 1755-80 on land originally granted to the Earl of Bedford in 1552 for services to Edward VI.

24

Egyptian influence on a bench of the 1870s, near Albert Bridge on Chelsea Embankment.

These days most mews have been converted into attractive homes. They were originally built as coach-houses.

Kensington was granted the title of *Royal Borough* by Queen Victoria in 1901 and amalgamated with Chelsea in 1965.

(above) This modest monument to a gentleman unnamed on his plaque is in Pickering Place, tucked away behind St. James's.

Traditional narrow boats, built to be able to pass through the locks of England's extensive canal system, make delightful homes on Regent's Canal in north London.

BANHAM
071
385 3322
28
29

left) The pastel paintwork of these terraced houses in Chelsea was probably added in the 1960s or 70s.

(above) Giles Gilbert Scott's classic telephone kiosk. This design was first seen on London's streets in 1927.

Even where space is at a premium the British house-owner (not just the Londoner) will make a splash of colour if he can.

Formal street furniture in Regent Street; completed by John Nash in 1816, all the properties in this famous thoroughfare are owned by the Crown Estate.

(left) This lamp-post with a piscatorial theme in bright colours is on The Embankment. The street furniture of London changes from one part of town to the next, a reflection of the fact that there has never been any real central control over planning.

(right) This elegant terrace is in Sumner Place, South Kensington. The area became fashionable as soon as William III instructed Christopher Wren to rebuild Kensington Palace. It remains one of London's most desirable residential districts.

(next page) The red-brick terrace with white decorative features and sash windows is very typical of south London. Whole districts of this type of building sprung up in the suburbs in the late 19th and early 20th centuries.

9
10
11
12

ove) Many of the apartment conversions of the East End and
th bank of the Thames are in former warehouses and industrial
ldings which until the second half of the 20th century were still

(right) Graffiti adorns a wall in the East End, near Brick Lane, another reminder that, like all big cities, London is not only history and elegant buildings.

SCLATER ST E.1

Londoners have learned to love their river. This development of flats at the south side of Battersea Bridge opened in 2005 and is built on a site formerly occupied by a brewery which stood derelict for many years. As well as providing beautiful river views, these large developments inevitably add to local traffic congestion.

London at Work

The familiar double-decker Routemaster bus has been a commuters' favourite and a London icon for over 50 years, but has now all but disappeared from the city's streets.

In the early 19th century a quarter of all Londoners worked in the docks or for other industries connected with shipping. Today a much higher proportion than this work in service sectors and there is little manufacturing at all left in and around the capital city. In the mid 1970s 700,000 people commuted into the City yet 30 years on this number has halved. What brings about these shifts in working practice?

In Roman and medieval times defence was the imperative. The citizens had to be able to withdraw into the protection of the city walls and be self-sufficient. Old London had its butcher and baker and candlestick maker and easy access to all the food its inhabitants needed but still the Romans saw the need to trade with other parts of Britain and with other countries. They felt the need for access to the goods, perhaps more luxuries than necessities, that they could not obtain locally. By medieval times London was one of Europe's main centres of commerce.

The first Elizabethan age, a golden era of English aggrandisement through international trade and exploration, coincided with London's first documented population explosion. Between 1565 and 1605 the population almost doubled to 155,000. In a royal proclamation of 1580 Queen Elizabeth I wrote: "...there are such great multitudes of people brought to inhabit in small rooms, whereof a great part are very poor, yea, must live by begging, or by worse means...heaped up together." One hundred years later and the old distinction between London city in the east and Westminster to the west had all but disappeared and by 1750 the population had reached 650,000, passing 1 million by the end of the century.

Mid-Victorian London was one of the world's richest cities but it was overcrowded, polluted, dark and dangerous. Living and working conditions for the poor were horrendous. The building of new bridges in the 1700s and 1800s had done much to ease the flow of humanity around the capital but it was the development of the railways from the 1830s which had the greater effect: the commuter age had begun. A quiet village like Wimbledon, then in Surrey and some 7 miles from Hyde Park Corner, was connected by rail (the Vauxhall – Woking line) in 1838; by 1861 its population had almost doubled to 4,644, rising to 9,067 in 1871 and 15,949 a decade later. If 18th and 19th century London was built upon the labour of the poor, the city of the last 100 years was surely built on the toils of the commuter.

By the outbreak of World War II London's population had reached 8.6 million but by the census of 1981 it was down to 6.7 million as Londoners moved to the suburbs. Urban regeneration and sustained immigration meant that by 2005 the level was back up to 7.5 million. After the devastation of the war years London was slowly rebuilt but its days as the world's greatest trading centre were in decline. Trade with the old Commonwealth countries was reducing, manufacturing industries were being challenged by cheaper, foreign producers and by the 1960s unemployment was rising. In rapid succession London's docks were closed as shipping moved on to containerisation. The immediate effect of the demise of the docks was the loss of vitality to local communities and at about this time the Greater London Council instigated a policy of encouraging people to return to the town and to reverse the exodus to the suburbs. Controls on building in the "green belt" around London were tightened and grants were given to homeowners to improve old properties and to businesses to relocate into deprived and run-down areas. Today the results can be seen all over London, from the gleaming towers of Canary Wharf to the "gentrified" former slums of Islington.

In 1961 London had a workforce engaged in manufacturing of 1.6 million; by 1991 this had fallen to a little over 300,000. This was to some extent a reflection of what was happening throughout the country but in London the decline was more extreme. London has lost not only its "sunset industries" such as textile manufacturing and shipbuilding, but also many firms in growing sectors, for whom the high cost of labour and premises as well as the congested transport system are no longer acceptable nor necessary. Firms have moved away to take advantage of cheaper land and labour, a better transport system and tax incentives.

Napoleon called the British "a nation of shopkeepers". Londoners certainly knew about conspicuous consumption as far back as records go. The permanent secure shop, as opposed to moveable market-stall, has been a feature of the townscape since medieval times and the High Street today offers employment to tens of thousands of Londoners. A noticeable change in recent decades has been the spread of chain stores, whose presence has led to an element of homogenisation, with one shopping street looking much like any other. The old-established department stores are an exception, as are the remaining specialist retailers and the markets.

London has had its markets since the earliest days but the variety today is immense. Most of the central food markets have been driven out to the suburbs where transport is easier. Covent Garden is now firmly on the tourist map, the flowers and vegetables having been moved out to Nine Elms; the Billingsgate fish market, established by the Thames in the 11th century, is now offices, but Smithfield can still surprise with its vast hall of butchers' shops with beef, pork and lamb carcasses suspended row upon row on gleaming meat-hooks. Petticoat Lane is one of the largest general markets and Portobello Road, in the now-fashionable area of Notting Hill, claims to be the world's largest open-air antiques market. Old Spitalfields Market on Commercial Street, a stone's throw from Petticoat Lane, was the location of a medieval hospital and priory founded in 1197. Set among fields on the edge of the City, it provided travellers with shelter or "hospitality", hence "spital fields". The markets tend to be operated by family-owned businesses or by sole traders who often work part-time at the market whilst holding down another "full-time" job.

Particular streets or districts have always had their specialities: the City for banking, Fleet Street for newspapers and printing, Clerkenwell for clock-, watch- and jewelry-making. The Strand and Aldwych were magnets for the law, Whitehall for government and Shoreditch and Tottenham Court Road for furniture-making and latterly for cheap electrical goods. Soho, once the home of London's strip-clubs and prostitutes (as well as some good jazz and excellent food) is now at the heart of the media world. Film, television and music provide employment and artistic outlet for thousands of Londoners. The great 1930s studios at Elstree, Ealing, Shepherd's Bush and Islington may not have kept up with Hollywood but London remains home to the world's finest special effects and post-production studios and continues to turn out world-class films, TV, music and advertising. Publishers of books, predominantly based in London, produce an immense annual outpouring of over

Workers in the "new City" of the Isle of Dogs crossing the old docklands river waters on their way to work at Canary Wharf. Until the 1980s nearly all financial service jobs were within the "square mile".

150,000 new titles. London also continues to be the home to a huge range of quality (and slightly less so ...) newspapers and magazines. Printing and publishing is now London's biggest single manufacturing sector.

Just as the electronic era heralded the diaspora of the newspapers from their established Fleet Street home to Wapping and the Isle of Dogs, so did it change forever the working patterns of the City of London. London banks, insurance companies, stockbrokers and traders employ around 700,000 people in the sector which constitutes the largest contributor to the economy of modern Britain. They were once confined to the square mile around the Bank of England but electronic trading has breached the City walls and many companies are now located either in Docklands or beyond the former northern and western City boundaries; an intrepid few have even ventured to the south side of London Bridge or out to the West End, unthinkable a decade or two ago.

Londoners have to be fed and watered. There are literally thousands of pubs, restaurants and take-aways in the capital. Together they constitute major employers although the low rates of pay attract a high proportion of untrained youngsters and temporary migrant labour. The same can be said for many of the other lower-paid jobs in hotels and tourism, transport, cleaning, security and health services. London now has a vast immigrant population, typically, at least in the first generation, forced to take on such work just to make a living. Like any city, London needs its police and firemen, hospital workers and teachers, prison guards and bus drivers, and not all of them are born and bred in the capital. Immigrants have brought their own specialities. In the 17th century the Huguenots brought silk-weaving. In the 1920s Greek Cypriots began settling in Soho and Camden, going into catering, hairdressing, clothing and retail. Carribean immigrants in the 1950s gravitated towards transport and hospital jobs, and the Irish, the largest single immigrant group in that period, went into construction and healthcare. Ugandan Asians in the 1970s became succesfull shopkeepers, (though their children are more likely to be doctors or IT consultants). Eastern Europeans in the 21st century are moving into building and decorating.

In the early 21st century traffic in London moves, on average, at 11mph, exactly the same speed as was achieved in the late Victorian era, before the invention of the motor car. London's authorities now try to discourage the use of the private car, through very high parking fees, the daily congestion charge for driving into central London, and the widespread use of "traffic calming" measures, including bus lanes and the closing of many streets to private cars. So today's London worker travels by foot or by bike, by bus or by train, by taxi or, of course, in the tube.

The first underground railway opened in 1863 and ran from Paddington to the City, a distance of 4 miles. The system now comprises 267 stations, 254 miles of track and around 500 trains carrying some 2.5 million passengers every weekday. For those who enjoy living in the suburbs or completely outside the capital, there are seven main railway stations connecting London with the rest of the country (and indeed the rest of Europe, via the Channel Tunnel) of which Victoria Station is the busiest, with almost 90 million passengers per year.

Lock & Co. in St. James's is an example of the old-established bespoke clothiers and outfitters to whom this part of London is still home.

Leadenhall Market, at the heart of the City, was given its elegant glass roof by the Victorians. It began life in the 1300s as a market held by farmers in the grounds of the Neville family's manor house, which had a lead roof.

Fleet Street remains synonymous with the press even though almost all of the newspapers have now moved out.

The 1960s market at Camden Lock has become a great attraction to young Londoners and tourists alike.

Petticoat Lane market is held on Sundays in Middlesex Street, once the boundary between London and the county of Middlesex.

Fish and game have been on sale at Leadenhall Market in the City since at least the 16th century.

Farmers' markets all around the city provide an outlet for fresh produce, as here beside the flower market in Colombia Road.

Portobello Road in Notting Hill is best known for its antiques but there are plenty of opportunities for refreshment.

A·T·R
SELF DRIVE
VAN & TRUCK HIRE
0207 537 0707
IN CINEMAS 29th APRIL
kaal
93CLUBS
BROCKWELL PARK
PARK
LIVE
THE STRANGLERS
MEHADRIN TNUPORT
Jaffa
Apples
FRAM
GHANA
FRESH PINEAPPLES
Freshtrop

(left) Brick Lane in the East End has had a market since the 1600s. This fruiterer now sells his produce alongside leather jackets, DVDs and saris in the midst of London's biggest Bengali community.

(above) Clothing on sale, aptly, in Petticoat Lane. The market was originally established to trade in pigs, with undergarments taking over in the 19th century. The prudish Victorians changed the name of the road to Middlesex Street but the former name has stuck.

This CamdenTown furniture shop tempts customers with an outdoor display of stripped pine.

A survival from the 19th century in the Spitalfields area, close to Petticoat Lane and Brick Lane.

London still has bakers with ovens on the premises. This one is in London's East End.

James Smith & Sons in New Oxford Street, "Umbrella, Whip and Stick Manufacturers", is one of the oldest shops in London.

(above) Portobello Road's antique stalls include specialists such as this camera-dealer, as well as purveyors of bric-a-brac.

(next page) Liverpool Street station was opened in 1874 on the site of Bedlam, the "lunatic asylum" founded in the 14th century.

Departures
GAMES & PSION
Old Broad Street
Liverpool Street
Bus Station
Bishopsgate
TAXIS
Reception
Tickets
Toilet
Babycare
Lift
BT Police

The Docklands Light Railway was an integral part of the new infra-structure enabling the regeneration of Docklands.

An atrium in the Canary Wharf complex provides a stark contrast to the old offices in the square mile.

London Bridge is the river-crossing to the City for commuters living to the south-east of town.

London may not yet be as cyclist-friendly as Amsterdam but there are still those determined to risk it.

(above) St. Pancras Station opened in 1868 and serves the Midlands. Charles Dickens said of the area where the station now stands: "A complete bog of mud and filth ... the stench of a rainy morning is enough to knock down a bullock".

(left) Not very long ago the skyline of east London bristled with cranes. Since the demise of the docks the few that remain are there for decoration.

(right) The Post Office Tower was completed in 1966 and stands 620 feet tall. The viewing tower, originally opened to the public, was closed after a bomb incident in 1975.

Portobello Road in North Kensington is on the site of a farm which was named after a Spanish colony in Central America, Porto Bello, captured by the English in 1739. It was originally a market reserved for horse-traders and is now open every day but Sunday.

London at Play

Not all that much has changed in the way Londoners and visitors to the city have entertained themselves over the past few centuries: some shopping, a visit to a gallery or museum, a drink in a pub, take in a show, a late meal, then on to the pleasures of the nocturnal metropolis, or back home to bed.

Where to shop? As may be expected London offers a vast array of temptation, from the great department stores such as Harrods, Harvey Nicholls, Peter Jones and Selfridges, to street markets offering anything from fresh flowers to DVDs. Harrods was founded in 1853 by a tea merchant in Knightsbridge, at that time on the outskirts of town. In 1908 Harrods boasted London's first escalator (with an assistant to offer smelling salts to any customer overwhelmed by the experience). Today, with over 300 departments and 4,000 staff it is a mecca for tourists who can spend over £1.5 million on a busy day.

Londoners patronise speciality shops for all sorts of goods. Floris in Jermyn Street could well be the oldest shop in London to have stayed in the hands of the same family at the same site. They have been selling perfumes here since 1730 and have held a royal warrant ever since the time of George IV. James Smith's umbrella and cane store is a later arrival (1830) and has been in New Oxford Street since the 1860s. Certain streets in London will always be associated with certain goods, such as suits from Savile Row, hand-made shoes or bespoke shirts from Jermyn Street, jewelry from Bond Street and musical instruments from Denmark Street ("Tin Pan Alley"). Charing Cross Road is the place for second-hand bookshops and South Moulton Street and Sloane Street for fashionable boutiques.

Almost every part of London is home to one or more markets and these can range from a modest fruit and vegetable barrow on a street corner to a vast general market which may have held its trading licence for many hundreds of years. Portobello Road is famous for antiques (and is also home to the splendid Electric Cinema), Columbia Road concentrates on plants and flowers, and Brick Lane (whose name harks back to medieval times, when bricks and tiles were manufactured here) offers leather jackets, cheap jewellery, second hand merchandise, bric-a-brac, furniture, tools, footwear, clothes, fruit and vegetables and a jellied eel stand.

If jellied eels are not to everyone's taste London has a great variety of fast foods, from the ubiquitous hamburger bars and pizza outlets to fish & chips, Indian, Chinese, Thai and many more ethnic options; there are sandwich bars and "greasy spoons" and stalls selling hot dogs on street-corners. The Romans introduced "taverns" *(tabernae)*, inns where travellers could find food and shelter, but the 19th century saw a real explosion of public houses ("pubs") designed to be no more nor less than drinking places. There had always been alehouses, offering beer brewed on the premises. In recent years, however, the majority of London pubs have started to become family-friendly and tempt the visitor with more than just "pub snacks".

The Theatre Royal, Haymarket, is the fourth theatre to stand on the site. The original one burned down in 1672, only nine years after its opening. This one opened in 1812 but the porch and pillars were not added until 1820 and 1831 respectively.

Restaurants as a place to enjoy the event rather than just find sustenance are a development of the 19th century. Rules, in Covent Garden's Maiden Lane lays claim to being London's oldest restaurant, beginning life as an oyster bar in the early 1800s. At first there were just simple inns and taverns, then coffee shops and chop houses. It was the spread of the railways in early Victorian times which led first to the building of hotels and later restaurants. The Café Royal in Regent Street and Kettner's in Soho both opened in the 1860s and are still going strong. Another traditional survivor is Simpson's in The Strand which dates back to 1828 and was the first restaurant to offer its roast meats from a trolly wheeled to the diner's table by the carver, who expected, and to this day still expects, a tip for his trouble.

The Design Museum opened on the site of a former warehouse at Butler's Wharf close to Tower Bridge in 1989.

Built in 1968, the Hayward Gallery, on the South Bank near Waterloo Bridge, is seen here with the London Eye in the background.

Traditional formal restaurants are still to be found but the gastronomic scene in London has developed beyond this and bears comparison today with any other world capital. Celebrity chefs with Michelin stars and prices to match seem able to fill their restaurants whatever the economic climate (or weather) yet the average Londoner is still more likely to be found eating out at his local Thai or Indian restaurant (the latter a great favourite after pub closing time) or enjoying a takeaway or just a bag of fish & chips.

Like most capital cities London offers a wide range of museums and galleries. The British Museum opened its doors in 1759, though only, in those days, to people applying for permission in writing. Today it is more liberal and has over 5 million visitors per annum to see not only its vast collection of antiquities but also the Great Square, transformed by architect Norman Foster into Europe's largest covered square. Amongst its treasures are the notorious Elgin Marbles, removed from the Parthenon in Athens and added to the collection in 1816. Until the mid-1990s the British Museum complex was also home to the British Library, which stores copies of every book ever published in the UK and currently holds over 10 million volumes. Because of space constraints it was moved to purpose-built premises in St. Pancras. When it first opened Prince Charles commented that the brick-built library, designed by architect Colin St. John Wilson, looked like "an academy for the secret police".

The British Museum was the first museum in the UK to open its doors to the public. Previously great collections had been put together by the monarchy, the wealthy and powerful, or by eccentric and intrepid travellers. Once the idea of museums took root many private collections were donated to form the core exhibits of the new museums. One such eclectic private collection was assembled by the architect Sir John Soane. He amassed a great number of paintings, manuscripts, sculptures, precious stones and antiquities which can be seen in situ in the three adjacent houses he owned in Lincoln's Inn Fields and which he gave to the nation in 1833, four years before his death. The museum displays, inter alia, Hogarth's eight *Rake's Progress* paintings, Bonaparte's pistols, Christopher Wren's watch and the sarcophagus of a pharaoh.

The Museum of London, on the other hand, is renowned not for the breadth of its collections but for being the world's largest and most comprehensive museum dedicated to a single city. It is on the edge of the Barbican development and was formed by a merger of the London Museum and the Guildhall Museum in 1976. The Museum of the Moving Image, located appropriately next to the National Film Theatre on the South Bank, opened under the arches of Waterloo Bridge in 1988 and covers its subject comprehensively, ranging from modern film and television

(left page top) Bankside power station designed by Giles Gilbert Scott opened in 1963, was decommissioned in 1981 and re-opened as Tate Modern in 2000 to house part of the Tate Gallery's collection of modern British art.

The Royal Albert Hall was originally called the Hall of Arts. Queen Victoria added the "Royal Albert" at the opening ceremony in 1871.

The replica of Shakespeare's Globe stands near the site of Richard and Cuthbert Burbage's original theatre, built in 1588-9.

The South Bank arts complex was erected for the Festival of Britain, an event designed to cheer up post-war Britain in 1951. The stark concrete structure contains venues for film, theatre, concerts and art exhibitions.

to 4,000 year-old puppetry. Other special-subject museums include the Bank of England Museum, HMS Belfast on the river, Freud's House, the London Dungeon and the Wimbledon Tennis Museum.

With the profits from the Great Exhibition of 1851 the Victorians purchased the land for not only the Albert Hall and Albert Memorial but also the great South Kensington museums. Side by side, a short walk from Harrods, sit the Natural History, the Science and the Victoria & Albert Museums. The architect of the Natural History Museum, Alfred Waterhouse, deliberately made the central hall reminiscent of a cathedral to remind visitors that they were seeing "the works of the Creator".

The major public art galleries include Trafalgar Square's National Gallery and associated National Portrait Gallery, the Tate Britain, (opened in 1897 with an art collection and money donated by sugar-baron Sir Henry Tate) and Tate Modern. Not publicly-owned but open to the public is the Queen's Gallery at Buckingham Palace, featuring art and artefacts collected by several generations of the royal family. Commercial art galleries are found throughout London with a particular concentration in Cork Street, just behind the Royal Academy, itself home for over 200 years to the annual Summer Exhibition.

London's first theatre, known simply as The Theatre, was built at Shoreditch in 1576. Up to this time plays had been performed in inns and alehouses or even in churches. The familiar design of our theatres, with their rows of galleries, is directly descended from the style of the old galleried inns, one of the last remaining examples being The George in Southwark, just a few minutes' walk from the site of Shakespeare's Globe. Pressure from the City authorities had shifted the burgeoning new theatreland over the river to Bankside in Southwark, outside the City's jurisdiction. Here the theatre flourished with famous names such as The Rose and The Globe (built from the timbers of The Theatre) opening between the brothels (known as the "stews") and alehouses and performing the exciting new works of Shakespeare and his contemporaries. It was not until the late 17th century that theatres began to open around Covent Garden, now home to the Royal Opera, and later the area around Shaftesbury Avenue in London's West End. Commercial theatre in the early 21st century is dominated by the musical, relatively undemanding fare for tourist and resident alike. There remain however a range of more serious theatrical venues, including The National Theatre at the Barbican, The Old Vic and The Royal Court as well as a plethora of smaller companies performing in pubs and studios throughout the capital. Opera is well-supported at The Royal Opera House, built in 1732 and originally called The New Theatre, and at The Coliseum, where the libretti are sung

In 1828 Simpson's in The Strand became the first restaurant to offer its roast meats from a trolly wheeled to the diner's table.

Londoners can now walk almost the whole length of the metropolitan Thames along the south bank of the river.

in English. Today around 50,000 jobs depend on West End theatre and it represents one of the UK's biggest tourist attractions as well as a civilising resource for the locals. As a net currency earner for the UK, West End theatre is similar in size to the entire UK advertising, accountancy and management consultancy industries - and bigger than the UK film and television industries.

Sport, both for participants and spectators, keeps many Londoners occupied throughout the year. The city has 13 professional football clubs and parks and playing fields resound to the shouts of amateur footballers or rugby players every winter weekend. There are golf courses, private and public, and many municipal parks have tennis courts available for hire at modest prices. Interest in tennis-playing always rises dramatically during the Wimbledon Championships fortnight. There are no longer many cricket clubs on the "village greens" of London but sales of cricket bats rose by 50% shortly after England won the ashes back from Australia in 2005. Interestingly, fishing is the activity which occupies the leisure time of more individuals than any other sport or hobby and oarsmen and sailors also enjoy the relatively calm waters of the Thames upriver from Putney. Equestrians are catered for with stables and riding schools in Hyde Park as well as the suburbs, and with the Olympics coming to London in 2012 it seems likely that interest in and opportunities for sport will only increase.

The sign above the door of one of London's few remaining bespoke shirtmakers shows a fox in hunting "pink".

London Zoo was opened in 1828 in Regent's Park and later included the world's first reptile house, insect house and aquarium.

Giraffes were first brought to the zoo in 1839 and started a new fashion in ladies' clothing printed to imitate animal skins.

Wimbledon Common in south west London has 17 miles of bridle paths and several local riding schools.

Rowing is popular on the Thames upriver from Putney Bridge where the annual Oxford and Cambridge boat race starts.

Venus Williams at Wimbledon; founded in 1868 the club's correct name is The All England Lawn Tennis and Croquet Club.

Tickets for Wimbledon's Centre Court are particularly hard to get. At the first championships there were no stands for spectators.

Fairs at Bankside have been a feature of London life for centuries. This one was held on the site of the new GLA building.

In winter the terrace of Somerset House at the northern end of Waterloo Bridge is turned into a public ice-skating rink.

London has literally thousands of pubs. Each has its individual sign which some social historians believe evolved to help the illiterate ... The Alma is seen here from the railway station in Wandsworth.

The Rising Sun is in Cloth Fair, Smithfield. Pubs in this area open early to serve workers in the meat market.

Hanging baskets crowd the windows of the Cask and Glass in Palace Street, Victoria.

The George, in Southwark, is the finest remaining example of the kind of galleried inn that would have been familiar to Shakespeare.

Many pubs survive primarily on neighbourhood trade, often serving only simple meals and snacks to the drinkers.

When weather permits the capital's pubs will spill out onto the pavements. The Bloomsbury is close to The British Museum.

The Albert in Victoria has managed to resist redevelopment.

The King & Keys in Fleet Street was once a favourite haunt of journalists.

The Queen of the Isle is on the Isle of Dogs, in Docklands.

The Punch Tavern reminds us of the traditional Punch and Judy shows.

The Old Bell offers ales from Nicholson's, a brewery founded in Maidenhead in 1840.

The Golden Lion is one of the more popular pub names; this one is in Chelsea.

Until the late 20th century El Vino in Fleet Street had a men-only policy at its bar.

The Goose is in Queen Victoria Street off Holborn on the fringes of the City.

The King's Arms is another extremely common pub sign; again in Chelsea.

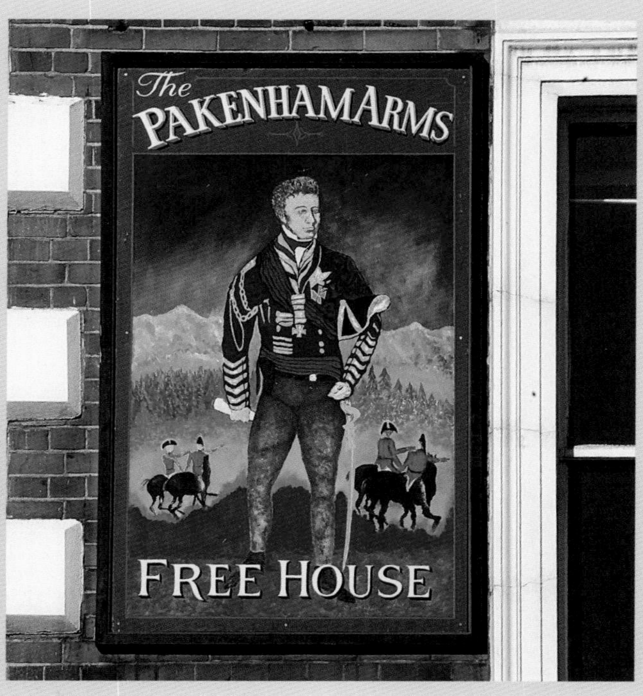

Many pubs are named after famous soldiers. The Pakenham Arms is in Clerkenwell.

Young's Ram brewery supplies Londoners with its renowned "ordinary" bitter.

Notting Hill Carnival, known locally simply as "Carnival", is now a major annual event attracting up to a million people per day to the two-day celebrations at the end of August. This area of west London was the destination for immigrants from the West Indies in the 1950s and, looking for a reminder of the more colourful life they had left behind in Trinidad or Jamaica, they started the carnival as a purely local event in 1966.

In 1976 closure was threatened after rioting and a high level of arrests. Since those days the licensing authority, the Royal Borough of Kensington and Chelsea, has worked hard to keep the event under control without destroying its spontanaeity and energy. It is still by far Britain's biggest street celebration and generally runs its course without serious disturbance. Music is loud, costumes are garish, and the newspapers and television love to get photographs of uniformed policemen dancing good-naturedly with scantily-clad revellers.

Vast quantities of Caribbean food and rum are served from the licensed vendor-stands and local cafes along the crowded streets around Ladbroke Grove and Westbourne Grove and some 250 temporary public lavatories are provided for visitors. Travelling in or around the area other than on foot becomes quite impossible.

B
B never too busy to be beautiful
LUSH

(above) Street entertainers are now a common sight on the piazza at Covent Garden. This unicyclist is performing in front of the portico of the "actors' church", St. Paul's, designed by Inigo Jones and completed in 1633. The opening scene of *Pygmalion* is set here.

(left) The area known as Covent Garden was until the 1530s the vegetable garden of Westminster Abbey. Charles I commissioned Inigo Jones to design the piazza which was roofed over by the Victorians. It was still used as a vegetable market until 1974.

The instantly-recognisable sight of Mick Jagger's lips which grace the front of the Rock Circus at the London Pavilion on Piccadilly Circus.

Every passing fashion can be enjoyed on the streets of the capital. Here two "punks" relax in the early evening sunshine.

Immigrants from the Indian sub-continent bring colour to London with their traditional silk saris.

The Piccadilly Arcade was built in the Regency style as recently as 1910. Its elegant neighbour, the Burlington Arcade, dates from 1819.

(above) Not many Londoners have the privelege of living on a boat on the river. This houseboat is permanently moored just west of Battersea Bridge, opposite Chelsea Harbour.

(above right) The London Eye was built to celebrate the millennium and was planned as a temporary structure on land leased for only five years. It stands 450 feet high and can carry 800 people at a time on a 30-minute trip or "flight".

(right) Many of London's restaurants have opened in buildings converted from completely different previous use. Conran's OXO tower was formerly a factory making the famous stock-cubes, and before that a power station.

Fireworks have been seen on the Thames at great celebrations for over 500 years. Here the river is lit up in magnificent style for the millennium festivities at midnight on December 31st 1999. This view is looking east from Vauxhall.

(next page) The West End is synonymous with theatre and Shaftesbury Avenue, laid out in the 1880s, is at the heart of "theatreland". The Lyric was the first theatre to open here, in 1888, followed by The Palace and The Apollo in 1901.

APOLLO
THE JOINT NEVER STOPS JUMPIN'!
FIVE GUYS NAMED MOE
SONG & DANCE DYNAMITE!
SIMON WARD
ROYCE MILLS
GILLIAN EATON
JUDY GRAHAM
SUE HODGE
Don't Dress For Dinner
LONDON'S LAUGHTER HIT
LYRIC BALCONY
LYRIC THEATRE
LYRIC THEATRE
Dress For Dinner
THE CHOREOGRAPHY BY CHARLES AUGINS IS BRILLIANTINE SLICK... NOT MANY SHOWS LEAVE YOU WISHING FOR MORE. "FIVE GUYS NAMED MOE" IS ONE OF THE FEW
BOX OFFICE NOW OPEN
G898 XOY

VALENTINE'S DAY
GLOBE
VALENTINE'S DAY
TONY SLATTERY
日本料理
花门
Kamon
JAPANESE CUISINE
& TEPPANYAKI
RESTAURANT
AMERICAN
STEAK
HOUSE
REQUEST
BUS STOP
NIGHT BUSES
Trocadero
KARAOKE
EVERY TUESDAY
A TASTE OF THE ORIENT
ALL UNDER ONE ROOF
FOOD STREET
KAMON
CHINA JOE

Each "pod" on the Millennium Wheel, now more commonly known as The London Eye, can hold 25 people, which means the wheel can transport 15,000 visitors per day for an unparallelled view across London and its suburbs.

Parks and Gardens

The first book about green London, *The City Gardener*, was written in 1722 by Thomas Fairchild, a nurseryman from the then rural area of Hoxton. He made horticultural history as the creator of the first man-made hybrid from two different sorts of flower. In his book he praises St. James's Park as possessing "an agreeable beauty ... which is wanting in many country places". But then he comments: "The quantity of ground, which now lies in a manner waste in Moorfields, might undoubtedly be made very agreeable, was it to be adorned after the same manner, and be as delightful to the citizens as St. James's Park is to the courtiers." Moorfields, in the northern part of today's City, had been preserved as playing fields for local residents as early as 1478 but 250 years later it had evidently dropped down the list of funding priorities. Other playing fields survived, such as Lincoln's Inn Fields, now London's largest enclosed square, and the old "pleasure gardens" of Vauxhall, Ranelagh and Battersea, the latter preserved as the large if rather dull Battersea Park. In Chelsea at the Physic Garden and Kew at the Botanical Gardens considerable areas of land were being saved from the builders through a passion for botany, but in general it was the Royal Parks which took precedence.

Ironically, in an era when hunting has finally been banned, it is to this very sport that Londoners owe the existence of the eight Royal Parks. The oldest part of Hyde Park was acquired by Henry VIII in the 1530s from the monks of Westminster Abbey on the dissolution of the monasteries (on Henry VIII's orders – an early example of compulsory purchase). Though the park now covers 350 acres the land then had an area of one hide (anything between 60 and 120 acres), hence the name. The king used it as a private hunting ground and so it remained until James I came to the throne and permitted limited public access. Charles I is the monarch who fundamentally changed the nature of the park in 1637 when he had it opened up to the public. It soon became the fashionable place to see and be seen by day though by night it was a haunt of robbers and highwaymen and became too one of the favoured locations for duelling. The Serpentine boating lake was added by Queen Caroline, wife of George II, in 1730, by diverting the Westbourne river, but it was the Victorians who added the statuary and flowerbeds and created the more formal atmosphere with which the modern visitor is familiar. Like most open spaces in London the park is still used: visitors are not kept off the grass and the huge open space is home to all sorts of public gatherings from huge concerts and demonstrations to the more modest crowds who gather on a Sunday morning to hear democracy's voice from the soapboxes of Speaker's Corner.

Londoners of today owe the existence of their Royal Parks to the obsession of previous kings, especially Henry VIII, with hunting. These red deer are in Richmond Park which was enclosed in 1637 by Charles I and is, at 2,350 acres, the largest of the Royal Parks.

The neighbouring Kensington Gardens were separated from the park by Queen Caroline to form the gardens of Kensington Palace. For most of the 18th century they remained closed to the public and when they were first opened it was only to "the respectably dressed". Queen Victoria, who was born in Kensington Palace and lived there until she moved to the newly-renovated Buckingham Palace in 1837, commissioned the Italian gardens and the Albert Memorial, recently restored to its former gilded glory. One of the best-loved features in the gardens is the bronze statue of J.M. Barrie's Peter Pan, standing on a pedestal covered with climbing squirrels, rabbits and mice. It was designed by Ivor Innes and erected in 1928. The Diana, Princess of Wales Memorial Playground and a seven-mile Memorial Walk, which continues through Hyde Park, Green Park and St James's Park, were opened in 2000.

Henry VIII's passion for hunting was also responsible for the creation of the 90-acre St. James's Park, almost a decade before Hyde Park. Originally the grounds of a leper hospital which was demolished by the king to make way for St. James' Palace, the park lies between the ancient Palace of Westminster (The Houses of Parliament) and the rather later Buckingham Palace. Henry drained the land and cut back most of the trees to create a deer park but less than a century later James I

A sunken garden at the palace of Hampton Court, one of the 50 palaces which once belonged to Henry VIII. The grounds include a vine planted in 1768, which still produces grapes.

had laid the park out as a formal garden and introduced a zoo and an aviary, the latter being remembered in the name of Birdcage Walk, the road running along the southern end of the park. Until 1828 the only person allowed to use this road, apart from the royal family, was the Hereditary Grand Falconer to the monarch.

Though technically outside London, Surrey's Richmond Park is, at 2,350 acres, the largest of the Royal Parks. With its high walls and gates this park was first enclosed for deer-hunting by Charles I in 1637. The park still retains the largest herd of red deer in England, as well as fallow deer and many ancient oaks at least as old as the park itself. Deep within the park is The Royal Ballet school, in the White House, built in 1729; Edward VIII was born here in 1894. Richmond Park's near neighbour, also in Richmond, Bushy Park is, at 1,100 acres, the second-largest of the royal parks. Lying north of Hampton Court Palace, the history of the park is inextricably linked to the palace and again it was Henry VIII who first enclosed it, in 1538, for hunting. One hundred years later Charles I was responsible for the taming of this area of fairly wild land, the reason this time being to improve the water supply to Hampton Court Palace. The park's most recognisable feature today is the mile-long chestnut avenue, designed by Christopher Wren as a formal approach to William & Mary's palace at Hampton Court.

Regent's Park or, more correctly, The Regent's Park, covers 487 acres if one includes Primrose Hill. Yet again it was first acquired by Henry VIII, this time from Barking Abbey in 1539, and its purpose was, of course, hunting. From the mid 1600s, by when much of its forest had been felled for shipbuilding, the park was turned over to agriculture. In 1811 the architect John Nash won a competition to develop the park as a "garden city" of fine houses in a rural setting. Nash's buildings, for instance Cumberland Terrace, today comprise some of London's most desirable housing. The park is now home to the famous open-air theatre, to a range of sports facilities and to the London Zoo.

Greenwich Park, at 183 acres, is the oldest of the Royal Parks. The area has been settled since Roman times but came into the ownership of the Duke of Gloucester, brother of Henry V, in 1427, to be enclosed by him some seven years later. Henry VIII was born at Greenwich and famously moved his court there from Westminster and once again was responsible for stocking the park with deer. Henry's daughters Mary and Elizabeth were both born here but it was Queen Anne, wife of James I, who commissioned Inigo Jones to build the palace now known as The Queen's House. Around 50 years later, in 1662, Charles II employed a French garden designer, Andre le Noitre, to create a formal garden with the Queen's House as its focal point. The previous year the king, who was also a great patron of science, had Christopher Wren start work on the Royal Observatory, which was completed in 1675 on the site of the former Duke of Gloucester's castle.

London also boasts several large areas of common land around its perimeters. Wimbledon Common comprises some 1250 acres used today for walking, riding, cycling and golf. From the early middle ages the manorial court would decide what

Ham House, once considered one of England's most luxurious houses, was within riding distance of Hampton Court Palace.

The National Trust now owns Ham House, with its formal gardens on the banks of the Thames. It was built in 1610.

Hampstead Heath's 790 acres were famous as early as the 17th century for the medicinal springs. The poets Keats and Pope lived in Hampstead and enjoyed the wilderness of the heath.

Hyde Park was acquired by Henry VIII as a hunting forest in the late 1530s. The 28-acre Serpentine was created in 1731 as a boating lake for the royal family.

Londoners like to *use* their parks and there is seldom any question of their being told to "keep off the grass". Green Park provides a popular lunchtime escape for local shop and office workers, politicians and civil servants alike.

the local tenants could do on the lands owned by the manor and not rented out for farming or other uses. In other words the commons were generally the poorest land in the manor. The locals acquired rights and protections under law because of their continuing use of these lands, which reduced the rights of the lords of the manor, preventing them, in theory at least, from selling commons for other uses. This system prevailed until the mid to late19th century. In the early 1800's a number of concerned local residents, angered by the Lord of the Manor Earl Spencer's proposal to enclose part of the common and build his new family mansion upon it, managed (just) to get his bill thrown out by Parliament. A descendant of his tried again in 1864, and lost again. An Act of Parliament was passed in 1871 "for the preservation of the whole of Wimbledon Common and Putney Heath, unenclosed, for the benefit of the neighbourhood and public". Golf was first played on the common in 1865 and when the Conservators took over the administration in 1871 they required "every person playing golf to wear a red coat or other red outer garment". To this day the same rule applies to all golfers on the common.

Hampstead Heath, in north London, extends to 790 acres, and from the 1830s to the 1870s the locals here had exactly the same struggles as their distant neighbours in Wimbledon to prevent their local Lord of the Manor, Sir Thomas Maryon, from selling off the heath to developers. Fifteen different parliamentary bills had to be defeated in the struggle to preserve the heath. At the same time, in Streatham, south London, local people turned out in secret to tear down gates and fences on the common as fast as the Lord of the Manor could put them up and in Plumstead and Forest Hill they marched in their thousands to save their commons.

Epping Forest, 13 miles north-east of Charing Cross is the East Enders' outdoor playground. A remnant of the woods which once covered south-east England, this was always a popular royal hunting area. Once again forest clearances and attempts at enclosure in the 19th century were finally fought off and an act of Parliament of 1874 placed the remaining 6,000 acres under the permanent control of the Corporation of London "for the enjoyment of the people forever".

Smaller areas of common land or village greens abound in most parts of suburban London and where there is no common there is often a municipal park. The Victorians were great park-builders, seeing open spaces as a critically-important part of the urban environment. Laid out in 1842 to a design by James Pennethorne, Victoria Park (London E3) was the first Victorian park to be owned by the public. Designed for recreational use, it became at once the great attraction of the East End. Today many municipal parks are shabby and under-used but there remain some good ones, including Queen's Park, East Ham, Hall Place Gardens, Sidcup, Battersea Park and Highgate Woods. Dulwich Park and Wimbledon's Cannizaro Park are renowned for their displays of rhododendrons, surpassed only by the magnificent Isabella Plantation in Richmond Park.

London's 19th-century cemeteries also provide some fine rustic walks and havens for wildlife, including the ubiquitous urban fox. The mid-Victorian part of Highgate is now open again, as well as the newer graveyard over the road which is best known for the monumental tomb of Karl Marx but is otherwise much less interesting than the older area. Cemeteries such as those at Kensal Green, Nunhead, West Norwood and Abney Park are charming and atmospheric and good places to sit quietly and contemplate. In the City, Bunhill Fields was first set aside as a cemetery during the Great Plague of 1665. It seems that the ground was never consecrated and so it became a popular burial place for non-conformists, who were banned from being buried in churchyards because of their refusal to use the Church of England prayer book. Bunhill Fields became known as "the cemetery of Puritan England". It is still possible to walk through it and find monuments to John Bunyan, Daniel Defoe and William Blake, as well as to members of the Cromwell family.

The Chelsea Physic Garden was founded in 1673, as the Apothecaries' Garden, a place to train apprentice apothecaries to identify useful plants. The location was chosen as the neighbouring river created a warmer microclimate enabling the propagation of many non-native plants (including the largest outdoor fruiting olive tree in Britain) and provided some protection against the British winters. By the 1700s an international botanic garden seed exchange system had been introduced, which continues to this day. Seed sent from the Chelsea Physic Garden to James Oglethorpe in Georgia in 1732 led to the subsequent growth of the US cotton industry.

The original Kew Gardens, properly known as The Royal Botanic Gardens, were created for Augusta, Princess of Wales in 1759 around her home, Kew Palace, with the assistance of Sir William Chambers. He was influenced by oriental gardening and designed the Chinese pagoda in the grounds. Queen Augusta's son, George III extended the gardens, which were landscaped by Capability Brown in the 1770s. The estate was acquired by the nation in 1841 and enlarged for the scientific study of horticulture, with many of its rare specimens being sent from all parts of Britain's then burgeoning Empire. Kew now contains the world's largest collection of plants, with tropical and sub-tropical specimens kept in appropriate conditions in magnificent Victorian glasshouses. There is a research library with over 125,000 monographs, an important seed-bank, and the Orangery, built in 1761, has now been converted into a museum and bookshop. The range of facilities and the impressive Victorian formality of the gardens, together with their sheer size, set Kew apart as a popular destination for anyone interested in gardening. The Royal Botanic Gardens were designated a World Heritage Site by the United Nations in 2003.

(next page) Even on relatively small boats there is space enough to create colourful gardens. Fortunately for the gardeners most of these narrow-boats, in north London's Little Venice, on the Regent's Canal, will never leave their moorings.

The Chelsea Physic Garden was established by the Apothecaries Company in 1676 to train its apprentices in the use of plants.

There is a serious aspect to Kew Gardens which does not prevent the visitor from enjoying the rural delights of its bluebell woods.

The Royal Botanic Gardens (Kew Gardens) occupy 300 acres. The Palm House by Decimus Burton was completed in the 1840s.

(right) Autumn in Kensington Palace Gardens, which was annexed from Hyde Park by Queen Caroline in the early 18th century.

Hampton Court was built by Thomas Wolsey, then Archbishop of York, in 1514 but given 15 years later to Henry VIII. The extensive grounds border the Thames, include Tudor-style formal gardens, and are the venue for an annual flower-show.

The Spencer family, then Lords of the Manor, tried to enclose and develop Wimbledon Common in the mid 1800s.

An Act of Parliament of 1871 now preserves the 1200-plus acres of Wimbledon Common "for public enjoyment".

Green Park (above) and its neighbour St. James's Park extend from Piccadilly to the Palace of Westminster.

Kensington Gardens are adjacent to Kensington Palace, which was built as a country mansion in the mid-17th century.

The lake in St. James's Park was laid out in the second half of the 1600s by the gardner who designed the grounds at Versailles.

St. Botolph's Church, Aldgate, has stood on this site in the City since at least 1115 and has retained a small but charming garden.

In 1811 John Nash won the competition to redevelop the wilderness of Regent's Park into a *rus in urbe.*

The Isabella Plantation is a botanic and wildlife enclave within Richmond Park and is famed for its spring displays of rhododendrons and azaleas.

Richmond Park, at over 2,300 acres, is the largest of the Royal Parks. It was first enclosed as a hunting reserve by Charles I in 1637, though his predecessors had doubtless also hunted there when staying at the nearby Hampton Court Palace. The park today is home to England's biggest herd of red deer and a smaller number of fallow deer. Each year the herd is culled and the venison distributed at the discretion of the Queen. The antlers, shed naturally each year are auctioned off for use in furniture-making. The author is the proud owner of a chandelier made of antlers from Richmond Park.

In the centre of the park are the Pen Ponds, built in the 18th century to offer fishing for pike, bream, carp and roach and the whole area is now a Site of Special Scientific Interest. The park is accessible by car but only along perimeter roads and the gates are locked at sunset every night. It is popular with walkers, joggers, golfers, and cyclists. The park has many miles of bridle paths, a number of polo-fields, and riding schools outside several of its gates, so is a great attraction for local riders. Ham House stands just beyond the western boundary of the park.

Photographer´s Note

Some thoughts on Photography

For me photography is essentially about trying to recreate what it felt like to be in a particular place at a particular time. Images that I have taken in the past invariably remind me of what it felt like to be there and what I felt like at that time. In very general terms, one of the functions and skills of an artist is the ability to find an aesthetic method of expressing feelings through images and sharing them with the world.

Compared to the skills you need to draw and paint, photography is relatively easy but just as satisfying artistically. Although technical understanding is an essential component in picture taking, I prefer to approach photography from a design point of view: in the same way that a painter deals with shapes, tones and textures on canvas, the photographer deals with shapes, tones and textures through the lens. The first priority is to consider the relationship of the essential design elements within a subject: line, shape, tone, space, pattern and texture, all the components that go to make up a two-dimensional image. As experience develops the ability to organise these relationships becomes intuitive. The second priority is to consider the technical requirements to achieve those aims in a picture. One useful tip in drawing and in picture taking is to look at the space between objects (negative shapes) as well as the objects themselves (positive shapes). In two-dimensional terms the negative shapes have equal value when composing images.

I love El Grecoesque images where the sky is full of foreboding and the landscape itself is bathed in bright sunshine (see the Alma pub on page 126). However, you can't be that lucky all the time, and one thing that I have learned through experience is to always take a picture. Waiting for "perfect" light is nonsensical, as you can take good images in almost all conditions. A successful photographer reacts to the environment he or she is in, rather than trying to impose preconceived ideas on a situation.

Although the light may not always be what you would like, you do need to think about the direction of light and to understand how its quality varies at different times of the day and in different seasons. Luck is important, but you can create your own luck by careful planning. Having a map and being able to work out where the sun will be at a particular time of day is essential. Photographs taken between 10 a.m. and 4 p.m. in summer on sunny days are usually disappointing: with the sun directly overhead, shadows are short (or non-existent) and the scene looks flat and uninteresting. Moreover, the colours are de-saturated.

I prefer to shoot early in the morning, but only because I don't mind getting up. In fact, evening light can be better as particles in the atmosphere build up during the day and can provide a softer, less contrasty result. Shooting into the light often yields great results, but be careful to keep the direct sun off the front element of the lens.

I use filters as little as possible. Apart from uv filters for lens protection, all the photographs in this book were taken without filters. This is a matter of personal preference. Filters have many uses: for example, they can overcome the limitations inherent in film emulsion by reducing contrast or warming up a cold scene. But they also increase the number of decisions that you have to make. Having less choice allows you to concentrate on producing the best result you can with the resources available.

I have recently "gone digital" and about 50 photographs in this book have been taken with a Kodak DCSProSLR/n 35mm camera. The great advantage of this camera at the present time is that it is full 35mm frame. So all the lenses perform as they were intended for film. What bliss to be able to correct colour on the computer! The downside is not having an original transparency to refer to for colour balance in the scanning and printing process. However, the technology is now in place to ensure, with colour profiles, calibrated screens etc., that colour is maintained throughout the chain of command from camera to printed page. I always burn the raw files on to a non re-writable CD so that I have a "camera original" of sorts that can't be changed.

A key element in successful image-making is to be open-minded. Having too fixed an idea of what one is trying to achieve before starting can be detrimental. Look at alternatives and don't be afraid of making mistakes. A flexible attitude, combined with an intuitive artistic approach and good technique, is the key to successful photography. This is even more possible now with the advent of digital technology and the low cost of taking a large number of pictures. Practise makes perfect! ■

6
Nikon FE
28mm PC Nikkor
f8, 1/15th
Velvia 50

7
Nikon FE
28mm PC Nikkor
f8, 1/60th
Velvia 50

7
Hasselblad
80mm Planar
f8, 1/125th
Velvia 50

8
Minolta
80-200/2.8
f5.6, 1/125th
Provia 400

8
Hasselblad
80mm Planar
f8.5, 1/60th
Velvia 50

9
Hasselblad
80mm Planar
f4, 1/2 sec
Velvia 50

9
Kodak DCS Pro
Nikon 28-70/2.8
f6.7, 1/4 sec
Digital 160

9
Minolta
80-200/2.8
f5.6, 1/60th
Velvia 50

10
Minolta
80-200/2.8
f8, 1/125th
Velvia 50

11
Hasselblad
80mm Planar
f8, 1 sec
Velvia 50

12
Kodak DCS Pro
Nikon 80-200/2.8
f11, 1/180th
Digital 160

12
Kodak DCS Pro
Nikon 28-70/2.8
f8, 1/125th
Digital 160

13
Kodak DCS Pro
Nikon 28-70/2.8
f5.6, 1/180th
Digital 160

13
Minolta
28-70/2.8
f8.5, 1/125th
Velvia 50

14/15
Nikon FE
28mm PC Nikkor
f8, 1/60th
Velvia 50

16
Minolta
80-200/2.8
f8.5, 1/125th
Velvia 50

16
Minolta
80-200/2.8
f5.6, 1/30th
Velvia 50

16
Linhof 6/17
90mm S.Angulon
f8, 1/30th
Velvia 50

17
Hasselblad
80mm Planar
f8, 1/60th
Velvia 50

18/19
Minolta
28-70/2.8
f5.6, 1/4 sec
Velvia 50

20
Hasselblad
150mm Sonnar
f8, 1/30th
Velvia 50

21
Kodak DCS Pro
Nikon 80-200/2.8
f8, 1/500th
Digital 400

21
Minolta
28-70/2.8
f8, 1/30th
Velvia 50

21
Hasselblad
50mm Distagon
f8, 1/60th
Velvia 50

21
Hasselblad
80mm Planar
f11, 1/60th
Velvia 50

22
Kodak DCS Pro
Nikon 80-200/2.8
f11, 1/125th
Digital 160

22
Linhof 6/17
90mm S.Angulon
f8, 1/4 sec
Velvia 50

22
Hasselblad
80mm Planar
f8, 1/125th
Velvia 50

22
Minolta
80-200/2.8
f4, 1/125th
Velvia 50

23
Minolta
28-70/2.8
f5.6, 1/90th
Velvia 50

23
Linhof 6/17
90mm S.Angulon
f22, 1/15th
Velvia 50

24
Minolta
80-200/2.8
f5.6, 1/125th
Velvia 50

25
Hasselblad
150mm Sonnar
f8, 1/60th
Velvia 50

26
Minolta
28-70/2.8
f8, 1/60th
Velvia 50

27
Minolta
80-200/2.8
f8, 1/125th
Velvia 50

28
Minolta
28-70/2.8
f8, 1/125th
Velvia 50

29
Hasselblad
50mm Distagon
f8, 1/60th
Velvia 50

30
Hasselblad
80mm Planar
f8, 1/125th
Velvia 50

31
Minolta
80-200/2.8
f5.6, 1/125th
Velvia 50

31
Minolta
80-200/2.8
f4, 1/125th
Velvia 50

31
Minolta
28-70/2.8
f8, 1/60th
Velvia 50

32/33
Nikon FE
28mm PC Nikkor
f8.5, 1/125th
Velvia 50

34
Hasselblad
150mm Sonnar
f8.5, 1/125th
Velvia 50

35
Minolta
80-200/2.8
f5.6, 1/125th
Velvia 50

36/37
Hasselblad
50mm Distagon
f8, 1/125th
Velvia 50

38
Minolta
80-200/2.8
f4, 1/250th
Velvia 50

38
Kodak DCS Pro
Nikon 28-70/2.8
f2.8, 1/350th
Digital 160

38
Hasselblad
80mm Planar
f8, 1/125th
Provia 100

39
Minolta
80-200/2.8
f4, 1/250th
Velvia 50

40
Hasselblad
80mm Planar
f4, 1/125th
Provia 100

40
Minolta
80-200/2.8
f5.6, 1/250th
Velvia 50

40
Linhof 6/17
90mm S.Angulon
f8.5, 1/30th
Velvia 50

41
Linhof 6/17
90mm S.Angulon
f5.6, 1/15th
Velvia 50

41
Nikon FE
28mm PC Nikkor
f8, 1/125th
Velvia 50

41
Hasselblad
80mm Planar
f8, 1/125th
Velvia 50

42
Minolta
80-200/2.8
f5.6, 1/125th
Velvia 50

43
Hasselblad
80mm Planar
f8.5, 1/125th
Velvia 50

44
Minolta
80-200/2.8
f4, 1/250th
Velvia 50

45
Minolta
80-200/2.8
f4, 1/30th
Velvia 50

46
Linhof 6/17
90mm S.Angulon
f8.5, 1/15th
Velvia 50

46
Kodak DCS Pro
Nikon 80-200/2.8
f9.5, 1/125th
Digital 160

46
Minolta
28-70/2.8
f11, 1/125th
Velvia 50

47
Hasselblad
80mm Planar
f8.5, 1/125th
Velvia 50

48/49
Linhof 6/17
90mm S.Angulon
f11, 1/15th
Velvia 50

50
Hasselblad
150mm Sonnar
f8, 1/60th
Velvia 50

51
Kodak DCS Pro
Nikon 80-200/2.8
f5.6, 1/1000th
Digital 160

52
Nikon FE
28mm PC Nikkor
f8, 1/125th
Velvia 50

52
Kodak DCS Pro
Nikon 80-20/2.8
f8, 1/350th
Digital 160

53
Kodak DCS Pro
Nikon 28.70/2.8
f9.5, 1/180th
Digital 160

53
Kodak DCS Pro
Nikon 80-200/2.8
f9.5, 1/125th
Digital 160

54
Kodak DCS Pro
Nikon 80-200/2.8
f8, 1/750th
Digital 400

55
Hasselblad
80mm Planar
f5.6, 1/125th
Velvia 50

56
Kodak DCS Pro
Nikon 80-200/2.8
f4.8, 1/60th
Digital 160

56
Hasselblad
250mm Sonnar
f8, 1/60th
Velvia 50

56
Kodak DCS Pro
Nikon 80-200/2.8
f4.8, 1/60th
Digital 160

56/57
Minolta
80-200/2.8
f5.6, 1/30th
Velvia 50

58
Kodak DCS Pro
Nikon 28-70/2.8
f8, 1/125th
Digital 160

59
Minolta
28-70/2.8
f4, 1/30th
Velvia 50

60/61
Minolta
80-200/2.8
f8, 1/125th
Velvia 50

62
Minolta
28-70/2.8
f5.6, 1/125th
Velvia 50

62
Minolta
80-200/2.8
f4, 1/125th
Velvia 50

63
Hasselblad
80mm Planar
f8.5, 1/125th
Velvia 50

64
Hasselblad swcm
38mm Biogon
f8.5, 1/125th
Velvia 50

64
Kodak DCS Pro
Nikon 80-200/2.8
f4, 1/1500th
Digital 160

65
Hasselblad
38mm Biogon
f8, 1/15th
Velvia 50

66
minolta
28-70/2.8
f5.6, 1/30th
Velvia 50

67
Linhof 6/17
90mm S.Angulon
f8.5, 1/60th
Velvia 50

68/69
Minolta
28-70/2.8
f8, 1/125th
Velvia 50

69
Linhof 6/17
90mm S.Angulon
f5.6, 1/30th
Velvia 50

69
Linhof 6/17
90mm S.Angulon
f5.6, 1/4sec
Velvia 50

70
Nikon FE
28mm PC Nikkor
f8, 1/8th
Velvia 50

71
Hasselblad
150mm Sonnar
f8, 1/60th
Velvia 50

72/73
Hasselblad swcm
38mm Biogon
f8, 1/125th
Velvia 50

74
Minolta Dimage
28-200/3.5
f8, 1/250th
Digital 100

75
Minolta
80-200/2.8
f8, 1/125th
Velvia 50

76
Hasselblad
50mm Distagon
f8, 1/125th
Velvia 50

77
Minolta
80-200/2.8
f5.6, 1/250th
Velvia 50

78/79
Kodak DCS Pro
Nikon 28-70/2.8
f5.6, 1/250th
Digital 160

80
Hasselblad
150mm Sonnar
f8.5, 1/125th
Velvia 50

81
Kodak DCS Pro
Nikon 80-200/2.8
f4, 1/500th
Digital 160

82/83
Hasselblad
50mm Distagon
f8, 1/125th
Velvia 50

84
Nikon FE
28mm PC Nikkor
f8, 1/125th
Velvia 50

84
Kodak DCS Pro
Nikon 80-200/2.8
f2.8, 1/30th
Digital 160

85
Minolta
80-200/2.8
f11, 1/60th
Velvia 50

86
Minolta
80-200/2.8
f5.6, 1/250th
Velvia 50

87
Minolta
80-200/2.8
f8.5, 1/60th
Velvia 50

88
Minolta
80-200/2.8
f8.5, 1/125th
Velvia 50

88
Nikon FE
28mm PC Nikkor
f8, 1/30th
Velvia 50

89
Minolta
28-70/2.8
f8.5, 1/125th
Velvia 50

89
Nikon FE
28mm PC Nikkor
f8, 1/60th
Velvia 50

90
Minolta
80-200/2.8
f5.6, 1/125th
Velvia 50

90/91
Nikon FE
28mm PC Nikkor
f8, 1/125th
Velvia 50

92
Minolta
80-200/2.8
f2.8, 1/500th
Velvia 50

92
Minolta
80-200/2.8
f5.6, 1/60th
Velvia 50

92
Minolta
80-200/2.8
f4.5, 1/30th
Velvia 50

92
Minolta
80-200/2.8
f4, 1/90th
Velvia 50

93
Minolta
28-70/2.8
f8, 1/125th
Velvia 50

94
Nikon FE
28mm PC Nikkor
f5.6, 1/125th
Velvia 50

95
Nikon FE
28mm PC Nikkor
f5.6, 1/60th
Velvia 50

96
Kodak DCS Pro
Nikon 80-200/2.8
f4.8, 1/90th
Digital 160

96
Minolta
28-70/2.8
f5.6, 1/125th
Velvia 50

96
Kodak DCS Pro
Nikon28-70/2.8
f8, 1/125th
Digital 160

97
Hasselblad
150mm Sonnar
f8.5, 1/125th
Velvia 50

98/99
Minolta
28-70/2.8
f4, 1/125th
Velvia 50

100
Minolta
80-200/2.8
f8, 1/125th
Velvia 50

101
Kodak DCS Pro
Nikon 80-200/2.8
f5.6, 1/90th
Digital 160

102
Kodak DCS Pro
Nikon 80-200/2.8
f5.6, 1/180th
Digital 160

103
Minolta
80-200/2.8
f8, 1/125th
Velvia 50

104/105
Kodak DCS Pro
Nikon28-70/2.8
f5.6, 1/750th
Digital 160

106
Nikon FE
28mm PC Nikkor
f8, 1/125th
Velvia 50

107
Kodak DCS Pro
Nikon28-70/2.8
f4.8, 1/45th
Digital 160

108
Kodak DCS Pro
Nikon28-70/2.8
f4, 1/1000th
Digital 160

108
Hasselblad swcm
38mm Biogon
f5.6, 1/8th
Velvia 50

109
Kodak DCS Pro
Nikon28-70/2.8
f6.7, 1/500th
Digital 160

109
Kodak DCS Pro
Nikon28-70/2.8
f4, 1/30th
Digital 160

109
Minolta
28-70/2.8
f4, 1/125th
Velvia 50

109
Kodak DCS Pro
Nikon28-70/2.8
f5.6, 1/500th
Digital 160

110
Kodak DCS Pro
Nikon 80-200/2.8
f5.6, 1/180th
Digital 160

111
Kodak DCS Pro
Nikon28-70/2.8
f4.8, 1/350th
Digital 160

112
Minolta
28-70/2.8
f5.6, 1/125th
Velvia 50

112
Kodak DCS Pro
Nikon28-70/2.8
f4, 1/30th
Digital 160

112
Minolta
28-70/2.8
f8, 1/125th
Velvia 50

112
Kodak DCS Pro
Nikon28-70/2.8
f8, 1/30th
Digital 160

113
Kodak DCS Pro
Nikon 80-200/2.8
f5.6, 1/90th
Digital 160

114	115	115	115	115	116	117	117	118	119	120	120
Minolta 28-70/2.8 f5.6, 1/30th Velvia 50	Kodak DCS Pro Nikon 28-70/2.8 f3.3, 1/350th Digital 160	Kodak DCS Pro Nikon 28-70/2.8 f5.6, 1/160th Digital 160	Linhof 6/17 90mm S.Angulon f32, 1/2 sec Velvia 50	Kodak DCS Pro Nikon 28-70/2.8 f5.6, 1/250th Digital 160	Hasselblad swcm 38mm Biogon f8, 1/125th Velvia 50	Hasselblad 50mm Distagon f8, 1/125th Velvia 50	Minolta 80-200/2.8 f5.6, 1/125th Velvia 50	Kodak DCS Pro Nikon28-70/2.8 f5.6, 1/500th Digital 160	Minolta 80-200/2.8 f8, 1/15th Velvia 50	Minolta 28-70/2.8 f5.6, 1/90th Velvia 50	Hasselblad 50mm Distagon f8, 1/125th Velvia 50

120	121	121	122	123	123	123	124	124	124	124	125
Kodak DCS Pro Nikon 28-70/2.8 f5.6, 1/250th Digital 160	Linhof 6/17 90mm S.Angulon f5.6, 1/60th Velvia 50	Minolta 80-200/2.8 f4.5, 1/125th Velvia 50	Kodak DCS Pro Nikon 80-200/2.8 f4, 1/1000th Digital 160	Minolta 80-200/2.8 f3.5, 1/60th Velvia 50	Minolta 80-200/2.8 f5.6, 1/125th Velvia 50	Minolta 80-200/2.8 f2.8, 1/125th Velvia 50	Linhof 6/17 90mm S.Angulon f5.6, 1/60th Velvia 50	Kodak DCS Pro Nikon 28-70/2.8 f6.7, 1/500th Digital 160	Minolta 80-200/2.8 f5.6, 1/250th Velvia 50	Kodak DCS Pro Nikon 28-70/2.8 f6.7, 1/500th Digital 160	Minolta 28-70/2.8 f2.8, 1/750th Velvia 50

125	125	125	126	126	126	127	127	127	128	128	128
Minolta 28-70/2.8 f5.6, 1/180th Velvia 50	Minolta 80-200/2.8 f5.6, 1/180th Velvia 50	Kodak DCS Pro Nikon 28-70/2.8 f5.6, 1/250th Digital 160	Sinar 6/12 65mm S.Angulon f11, 1/60th Velvia 50	Minolta 28-70/2.8 f5.6, 1/60th Velvia 50	Minolta 28-70/2.8 f3.5, 1/125th Velvia 50	Hasselblad 500 80mm Planar f8.5, 1/125th Velvia 50	Kodak DCS Pro Nikon 28-70/2.8 f8, 1/500th Digital 400	Kodak DCS Pro Nikon 28-70/2.8 f5.6, 1/30th Digital 160	Nikon FE 28mm PC Nikkor f8.5, 1/125th Velvia 50	Kodak DCS Pro Nikon 80-200/2.8 f4, 1/2000th Digital 160	Minolta 80-200/2.8 f5.6, 1/180th Velvia 50

128	128	129	129	129	129	129	129	130	130	130	130
Minolta 80-200/2.8 f5.6, 1/180th Velvia 50	Minolta 80-200/2.8 f5.6, 1/180th Velvia 50	Minolta 80-200/2.8 f4, 1/250th Velvia 50	Kodak DCS Pro Nikon 80-200/2.8 f4, 1/2000th Digital 160	Kodak DCS Pro Nikon 80-200/2.8 f6.7, 1/500th Digital 160	Minolta 80-200/2.8 f5.6, 1/250th Velvia 50	Kodak DCS Pro Nikon 80-200/2.8 f11, 1/500th Digital 400	Minolta 80-200/2.8 f5.6, 1/90th Velvia 50	Minolta 80-200/2.8 f2.8, 1/180th Velvia 50	Minolta 80-200/2.8 f3.5, 1/125th Velvia 50	Minolta 80-200/2.8 f2.8, 1/125th Velvia 50	Minolta 80-200/2.8 f4, 1/90th Velvia 50

131	131	132/133	133	134	135	135	135	136	136	136	137
Minolta 80-200/2.8 f5.6, 1/60th Velvia 50	Minolta 80-200/2.8 f2.8, 1/125th Velvia 50	Kodak DCS Pro Nikon 80-200/2.8 f4.8, 1/30th Digital 160	Kodak DCS Pro Nikon 80-200/2.8 f2.8, 1/250th Digital 160	Minolta 80-200/2.8 f5.6, 1/125th Velvia 50	Minolta 80-200/2.8 f4, 1/125th Velvia 50	Minolta 80-200/2.8 f8, 1/125th Velvia 50	Linhof 6/17 90mm S.Angulon f11, 4 secs Velvia 50	Minolta 80-200/2.8 f3.5, 1/125th Velvia 50	Hassleblad 500 250mm Sonnar f8, 1/15th Velvia 50	Hassleblad 500 150mm Sonnar f8, 4 secs Velvia 50	Hassleblad 500 80mm Planar f8, 10 secs Velvia 50

138/139	140	141	142	143	143	143	144	145	146/147	148	148
Sinar 6/12 65mm S.Angulon f8, 8 secs Velvia 50	Minolta 80-200/2.8 f5.6, 1/250th Velvia 50	Minolta 80-200/2.8 f3.5, 1/250th Velvia 50	Linhof 6/17 90mm S.Angulon f32, 1/2 sec Velvia 50	Minolta 28-70/2.8 f5.6, 1/60th Velvia 50	Minolta 28-70/2.8 f8, 1/60th Velvia 50	Linhof 6/17 90mm S.Angulon f32, 1/2 sec Velvia 50	Linhof 6/17 90mm S.Angulon f11, 1/15th Velvia 50	Minolta 28-70/2.8 f8, 1/60th Velvia 50	Linhof 6/17 90mm S.Angulon f11, 1/15th Velvia 50	Linhof 6/17 90mm S.Angulon f11, 1/15th Velvia 50	Hassleblad 500 50mm Distagon f8, 1/125th Velvia 50

Page	Camera	Lens	Aperture, time	Film
148	Linhof 6/17	90mm S.Angulon	f11, 1/15th	Velvia 50
149	Nikon FE	28mm PC Nikkor	f11, 1/60th	Velvia 50
150	Linhof 6/17	90mm S.Angulon	f32, 1/2 sec	Velvia 50
151	Hassleblad 500	50mm Distagon	f8, 1/125th	Velvia 50
151	Minolta	28-70/2.8	f5.6, 1/30th	Velvia 50
151	Linhof 6/17	90mm S.Angulon	f32, 1 sec	Velvia 50
152	Kodak DCS Pro	Nikon 80-200/2.8	f8, 1/125th	Digital 160
152	Minolta	28-70/2.8	f5.6, 1/30th	Velvia 50
152	Minolta	28-70/2.8	f5.6, 1/30th	Velvia 50
152	Hasselblad swcm	38mm Biogon	f5.6, 1/60th	Velvia 50
153	Kodak DCS Pro	Nikon 80-200/2.8	f4, 1/125th	Digital 160
154	Minolta	28-70/2.8	f5.6, 1/60th	Velvia 50
154	Minolta	28-70/2.8	f5.6, 1/125th	Velvia 50
154	Kodak DCS Pro	Nikon 80-200/2.8	f4, 1/180th	Digital 160
155	Minolta	80-200/2.8	f5.6, 1/125th	Velvia 50

Page Nr

Camera
lens
aperture, time
Film

Acknowledgements

I would like to thank all those involved in the production of this book: Cameron Brown for giving me the opportunity to get some more of my photographs into print and for his illuminating and informative text. Stefan Nekuda for his outstanding design and Ditz for her editorial work on both the pictures and the words.

This book is for Katy, Amy and Timothy.

Sam Lloyd